# UNBEATEN TRACKS IN ISLANDS OF THE FAR EAST

## Experiences of a Naturalist's Wife in the 1880s

ANNA FORBES

SINGAPORE OXFORD NEW YORK
OXFORD UNIVERSITY PRESS
1987

*Oxford University Press*

*Oxford   New York   Toronto*
*Petaling Jaya   Singapore   Hong Kong   Tokyo*
*Delhi   Bombay   Calcutta   Madras   Karachi*
*Nairobi   Dar es Salaam   Cape Town*
*Melbourne   Auckland*

*and associates in*
*Beirut   Berlin   Ibadan   Nicosia*

*OXFORD is a trademark of Oxford University Press*

*Originally published as* Insulinde *by William Blackwood and Sons 1887*
*First issued as an Oxford University Press paperback 1987*

*ISBN 0 19 588857 X*

*Printed in Malaysia by Peter Chong Printers Sdn. Bhd.*
*Published by Oxford University Press Pte. Ltd.,*
*Unit 221, Ubi Avenue 4, Singapore 1440*

Dedicated

TO

ISABEL, COUNTESS OF ABERDEEN

AS AN EXPRESSION OF THE WRITER'S ADMIRATION

OF HER LADYSHIP'S BENEVOLENT INTEREST

IN HER FELLOW-CREATURES

# PREFACE.

SINCE my narrative explains itself, I have little to say here beyond accounting for a certain resemblance in these pages to the latter part of the work issued by my husband last year. After I joined him, we shared for the most part the same experiences; but we looked upon them from an entirely different standpoint. Many of my own sex who might turn from 'A Naturalist's Wanderings' because of the admixture of scientific matter, may find some interest in reading my simpler account.

I have told my life as I lived it, with its interests and pleasures, its drawbacks and discomforts, neither romancing nor withholding. I may confess that I did not write these letters *en route*. For this I had neither time nor strength, as I was never one single fortnight free of fever after entering the tropics. The following pages are pieced together from letters actually written home, from my journal, and from recollections that can never be dimmed. I consider it an advantage to write when time has removed the exaggerations with which the mood of the moment might have distorted facts or influenced feelings; while I have also had opportunity for maturer consideration of, and authentic information on, many points.

It is with pleasure that I acknowledge my indebtedness to my sister Carrie, and my friend Mr D. M. J. James, Forres, without whose aid these pages had never reached their present form. The former has transcribed this little work throughout; and the latter, on a sudden call to me to join my husband in New Guinea, has taken my manuscript from my hands, entailing on himself the no inconsiderable labour necessary for the completion of a book even after the actual composition is accomplished.

ANNA FORBES.

Rubislaw Den, Aberdeen,
6th March 1886.

# CONTENTS.

## CHAPTER I.

## CHAPTER V.

## CHAPTER VI.

## CHAPTER VII.

## CHAPTER VIII.

## CHAPTER IX.

## CHAPTER X.

## CHAPTER XI.

## CHAPTER XII.

## CHAPTER XIII.

## CHAPTER XIV.

## CHAPTER XV.

## CHAPTER XVI.

# THE EASTERN ARCHIPELAGO.

## CHAPTER I.

EASTWARD HO !— COLOMBO — THE JAVA COAST — BATAVIA—
HOTEL LIFE — THE *SARONG* AND *KABIA* — A BATAVIAN
BREAKFAST — THE NEW TOWN — CHINESE PEDDLERS —
THE JAVANESE.

BUITENZORG, *April* 8.

YOU have doubtless long ago heard by tele-
gram of my safe arrival in the East; but you
must be impatient to learn some details of my
experiences.

Forty-one days after leaving England by the
Queensland mail we had passed through the
Sunda Straits, and were winding among the
Thousand Isles towards the port of Batavia.
Before reaching the Dutch Indies, I had a fore-
taste of tropical beauty in a day on shore at
Colombo in Ceylon; and partly because all was

A

so new to me, partly that we had been many
days at sea, I was perhaps the more ready to
receive the impressions of delight with which
my introduction is associated. But it was made
under particularly favourable circumstances.
Heavy rain had fallen in the night before we
landed; and as we rapidly drove through the
bright clean streets of novel architecture, past
natives familiar in pictures, by neat gardens
under the rich unwonted foliage in the scent-
laden air, my anticipations were more than
realised; and when towards evening we drove
back to the ship through the Cinnamon Gardens,
gazing on a picture of surpassing splendour as
the sinking sun diffused his rich colour in a
thousand hues over the sky, lit up the earth,
and mirrored his dying glory in a long crimson
gleam on the Lake, I ended a day not only of
unmixed satisfaction but of keen enjoyment.

After another fortnight at sea, it was pleasant
again to look on land; and all that last day of
the voyage we never wearied of standing, glass
in hand, watching on the right the amphitheatre-
like slopes of the Java coast, laid out in coffee-
gardens and rice-terraces, and on the left the
more distant, deeply indented coast of Sumatra.
The lovely islets which stud the ocean recalled

at once Max Havelaar's exquisite simile, where he speaks of "Holland's magnificent empire of Insulinde, which winds about the equator like a garland of emeralds." These islets we passed now so close as to see distinctly the forms of tropical vegetation, the huts, and even the dusky inhabitants; again at such a distance that we could only contrast the rich hues of their verdure with the deep blue of the sea. The coast of Java, nearer Batavia, presents a singular appearance : for miles into the interior it seems elevated above the sea-level scarcely more than the height of the trees that cover it, and nothing can be seen save the sea-fringe of vegetation in front of a green plain, behind which rise the hills of Bantam and the Blue Mountains, as the old mariners call the peaks of Buitenzorg.

It was already dark when we moored in the roads of Batavia, one of the greatest centres of commerce in all these seas, where rides a fleet flying the flags of all nations. H., who had returned to Batavia from a prolonged tour in Sumatra to meet me, now joined me, and took at once all responsibility. Transferred into a steam-tender, we approached the mouth of the long canal by which the town of Batavia is reached; and having passed on shore at the Custom House, where we had moored, we entered a carriage drawn by two fleet ponies of the famous Sumbawa breed. We sped on for some miles through what seemed an endless row of Chinese shops and dwellings, before which the occupants, visible in the lamplight as we flashed past, sat smoking at their ease. Thence we emerged into a more genial atmosphere, where trees margined the street, and brilliantly lighted residences and hotels with pillared marble fronts gleamed through the delicate curtains of foliage which intervened between them and the roadway.

Apartments were ready for me in the Hotel der Nederlanden, and there I remained some days; but as I found the heat very oppressive, we have come here to Buitenzorg, some thirty miles inland, and considerably above the sea-level, where the climate is much pleasanter.

But I must try to give you some idea of my first impressions of life in the East,—how different from Western life and ways you must come here fully to learn.

About 5.30 of the morning after my arrival, I was awakened by the rattle of cups in my verandah. Coffee was already there, but, except to notice that it was neatly served, I did not heed that refreshment, for curiosity and wonder at the scene before me. Hotels here are all rather similar in plan. Imagine a quadrangle, the front of which is isolated from the three other sides of the square by the carriage-ways which lead into the centre. In this front block is the reception-hall, fronted by a verandah. The verandah is paved with marble, and disposed in it are numerous small tables, chairs, and lounges. Towards evening it is brilliantly lighted, and is the resort of the occupants of the hotel before and after dinner. Passing from the verandah through the reception-hall, you find the dining-room extending back into the square. It is simply roofed, and flowers in pots and pendent creepers fill the open sides. A few bedrooms have place in this front block : they are perhaps cooler, and are generally occupied by bachelor gentlemen who permanently reside in the house. For my part, I prefer one of those out in the courtyard formed by the remaining three sides of the square, for these have each a verandah, furnished with a table and a lounging-chair, making as it were a parlour for the occupant of the bedroom behind. I could best picture these rooms by comparing them to a row of cottages ; but instead of a porch to each, imagine a continuous verandah the length of the row. They

arc of one storey; the floors are of flags, for
coolness, with mats thrown here and there, and
very simple furniture. The beds, however, are
the largest I have ever seen, and are curtained
top and sides with mosquito-screens : they are
not furnished with any upper sheet or covering.

My room was quite at the end of the row, and
had a verandah at the end, as well as in front, with
blinds drawing to the ground, which screened me
from the gaze of passers-by, but through which
I could easily see them. When I looked out
that first morning, the occupants of the various
" cottages " were just emerging, and, seating
themselves in their sleeping attire, sipped their
morning coffee. I had been told that the bath-
house was at the farther end of the square, and,
summoning all my courage, I set off, armed with
towel and sponge, to find it. Far down, I espied
a lady companion of the voyage, who had been
in Batavia before, and was therefore not so
bewildered as I. She explained to me the
Eastern mode of bathing, by having pails of
water poured over the head, otherwise I should
have been puzzled on entering the bath-room to
know whether I was expected to climb into the
large vat which stood there. The bath-rooms
are arranged so as to be unspoilable from splash-

ing : a wooden net-work, on which one stands, covers a floor of flags, and the water flows quickly out by a wide drain.  The manner of bathing is exceedingly refreshing, and is less fatiguing than a plunge-bath.   As I returned to my room, at every "cottage" door sat the occupants, the gentlemen lying back in their chairs, with their bare feet extended over the long ledges which are there for the purpose.  Ladies sat by them, and *baboos* and "boys" (male servants, waiters and valets, men of all ages, are "boys" here) hurried hither and thither; the bustle of day had already commenced.  Did you ever have a nightmare, the misery of which was that you imagined you were walking out in your night-dress ?  That was exactly my feeling ; and the fact that I wore a dressing-gown made me an object of greater curiosity and regard, so that it was with the utmost thankfulness that I gained the shelter of my own room.

All this publicity of private life is the effect of climatic influence.  The easy attitudes and *negligé* costumes I describe appear fitted for a high-walled garden, or a country retreat, not for a public hotel; but gradually one comes to feel that these habits are natural in the climate.

You have heard of the *sarong* and *kabia?*

You can recall the description which we read in
Max Havelaar, and which we thought so extraordinary : " Mrs Havelaar was dressed in a
long white gown or robe without waist-band,
which descended to her knees. Instead of a
respectable skirt, she wore underneath a piece
of dark linen, covered with flowers, which seemed
to be wrapped round her body and knees very
tightly." The *sarong* and *kabia* form the native
dress, adopted by European ladies for comfort
and convenience in the climate, and worn by
them as sleeping attire, as also during the day in
a richer form, in which the skirt is of costly stuff,
and the jacket of fine lawn muslin or linen,
daintily trimmed with lace or embroidery. It is
not worn when receiving formal visitors, and
young unmarried ladies are not expected to be
seen in it beyond their private apartments ; but,
with an apology for the liberty, it is worn almost
constantly, except in the evening, when every
one wears European costume for a few hours.
In this country part, I see some ladies take the
morning stroll in *sarong* and *kabia*, and I must
confess I envy them, they look so lightly clothed
and comfortable; and when the eye is accustomed
to the costume, it is really becoming. I am
actually, despite the amazement I experienced on

first seeing it, now inclined to say it is pretty.
"Describe it, then," you say. Yes; but how?
Imagine a piece of calico, two yards long, cut
from a web. Sew together the two raw edges,
and you have a petticoat, without band or hem.
Imagine it covered with floral patterns, or curious
devices of crawling creatures, or having a village
with houses and scenes from daily life depicted
on it, and you see a *sarong* or skirt. Put this
over your head, draw *all* the fulness in front,
and form of this a large plait; put round your
waist, to hold it firm and confine it, a cord with
a rich tassel depending, or a gay silk sash. Then
put on a *peignoir*, or dressing-jacket, of fine lawn
trimmed with lace; loosen your hair and let it
fall down your back; slip your stockingless feet
into Indian-looking pantoffles, with gilt or silver
embroidery, and with no upper heels, but very
high wooden ones. Take now a fan in your hand,
and promenade before your mirror, and you have
some idea of the figures which my surprised eyes
saw moving about the quadrangle of the Hotel
der Nederlanden on the first morning after my
arrival. After all, is it so extraordinary? The
European fashion at present is to have the dress
drawn towards the back until it is really difficult
to walk : all fulness of the skirt is disposed be-

hind. The arrangement of the *sarong* is simply this reversed, with the advantage that walking is not impeded. And how cleanly is the *kabia*. A lady puts on a fresh one twice or thrice a-day,— a frequency with which one could scarcely put a dress aside as soiled ; and the wearer always looks cool and at ease.

Gentlemen wear a very loose and untrimmed form of the *kabia*, and wide, gay-patterned *pyjamas*, as sleeping-dress, which they do not put off until it is time to dress for the day. They walk about the courtyard and even beyond for a short stroll, with the addition only of a short tweed shooting-jacket, and are very ludicrous figures as the wind blows out the loose garments like sails in a breeze. This dress does *not* become them !

Between 7 and 9 breakfast is laid out in the dining-room, and when it suits you, you enter : one of the many waiters brings coffee and eggs, and draws within reach a few of the numerous plates of sliced cold meat and sausage which are spread over the table. To one accustomed to an English breakfast, that offered here is very unappetising, but it is simply a go-between, and a good appetite awaits breakfast or tiffin at 12 or 12.30, when no one could complain of want

of substantials or variety. It is called by the
Dutch the "rice table." On a large soup-plate
you help yourself to rice offered on an immense
platter, and over this you put a few spoonfuls
of Malay curry, which has the appearance of a
pale yellow soup. Then in close succession are
offered fish, cooked in various ways, fried, stewed,
curried; fowl, likewise in different forms; stewed
beef, rissoles of pork, mince patties, fritters of
maize, omelette, fried eggs, various vegetables,
with many Eastern delicacies and piquant side-
dishes. To these, a small portion of each having
been taken, are added various condiments—
pickles, sliced cucumber, chili, chutnee—which
are offered prettily arranged on a large china
tray. Then the whole is mixed with spoon and
fork, the mixture having, I am told, a delicious
flavour not otherwise obtainable. I have not
yet tried it. I form a wall of rice between the
fish and the fowl, and allow most of the dishes
to pass. H. says I shall learn, however, to enjoy
the rice table soon.

Beefsteaks with fried potatoes follow this
course, fritters of pine-apple and other sweets
succeed, and the meal ends with coffee and
fruits. How very rapidly it is got through!
But one needs to be initiated how to proceed.

I noticed an English family who had come on shore from a passing vessel for the day, who really got almost nothing. They took a little rice and curry and a morsel of fowl, and proceeded to discuss these leisurely, refusing with a surprised air the many dishes offered. They then wished some of the good things which others had partaken of, but they had all disappeared into the courtyard towards the kitchens, and it was only on H.'s intervention that they were served with some beefsteak.

After this mid-day meal, all who are not forced by business engagements to return to town retire to rest, and silence like night falls on the house. No one is seen stirring : even the servants fall asleep in corners until about 4 o'clock. Then tea is brought, and along the " cottage " row the scene of early morning is repeated. One after another appears with towel on arm proceeding to the bath-houses, and about half-past 5 all are ready in European toilet for an evening stroll or drive, previous to dinner at 7.30. It seems that the fashion so long prevalent of ladies going out at this hour in demi-toilet is passing away, bonnets and close dresses being now in vogue ; but many still hold to the old fashion, and the effect is rather pretty as they promenade under the great avenues or flash past in carriages in the gathering dusk. Gentlemen, however, still go with uncovered heads.

Taking the opportunity of the comparative coolness of early morning and early evening, we saw not a little of Batavia during the few days of my stay. I call it a beautiful city, and you must not imagine it behind the world, for steam tram-cars puff along its streets. There is an old town and a new. The old town— close, fatal-climated Batavia of past days—lies near the strand, scarcely at all above the sea-level. A traveller dropped down here by chance might make a very good guess at the national-ity of the dominant power. Canals intersect the town in every direction; and dear are these placid water-roads to the heart of a Hollander, as to a Highlander his heather hills. On the banks of these are the Government offices, the Town-house, and the various consulates and banks; and round this European nucleus cluster the native village and the Arab and Chinese quarters. In this low-lying, close neighbour-hood, devoid of wholesome water, scorched in the day-time, chilled by the cold sea-fogs at night, the Eastern merchant of long ago re-sided as well as traded. Out of this, however, if he survived the incessant waves of fever, cholera, and small-pox, he returned home in a few years, the rich partner of some large house, or the possessor of a great fortune.

All this is changed now. The open salubrious suburbs of the new town can be reached by train in a few minutes. The King's Plain, which is a mile square, is flanked by fine residences standing among groves of trees. In this district the Governor-General has his official palace; and here are built the barracks, the clubs, the hotels, and the best shops, dotted along roads shaded by leafy hibiscus shrubs.

Not far from the Hotel der Nederlanden is the Harmonie, a fine club-house, the grounds of which presented a charming scene when I first entered. Brilliant moonshine made fairyland of the rich foliage, sweet heavy scents of tropical plants pervaded the air, a band discoursed faultless music, and hundreds of gaily dressed people moved to and fro between the lamp-glare and the dimmer moonlight, or sat playing or talking at small tables in Continental fashion.

Every morning we drove to the hospital, a large and splendidly conducted institution in a beautiful situation, to see an English friend of

H.'s, who was lying there. Coming back we generally met the children going to school,— little bands of them, with faces about as white as their garments. Girls wear simply a pinafore, or chemise if you will, of white starched muslin, over rather long drawers, white stockings, and long black boots. The effect is rather odd, and my impression on first seeing them was that a number were setting off to bathe still half-dressed. I was also much interested in watching the gay and busy scene on the canal near our hotel,—tiny barges, busy washers, and black bathers enlivening it from daybreak to sunset.

Batavia contains many thousands of Chinese inhabitants. Without this element, indeed, she might almost close her warehouses and send the fleet that studs her roads to ride in other harbours, for in every branch of trade the Chinaman is absolutely indispensable. Many of them possess large and elegantly fitted-up shops, filled with European, Chinese, and Japanese stores. Their workmanship is generally quite equal to European, and in every case they can far undersell their Western rivals. Numbers of a poorer class go about as peddlers, carrying all sorts of wares, from a silk dress to a linen

button, from a China service to a thimble.
When you emerge from the bed-chamber to
the verandah to sip your morning coffee, John
Chinaman is before you. His wares are already
undone. He presses you to buy with a persist-
ence to which at first you fall a prey, were it
only to rid you of his importunity. He makes
the most ridiculous overcharges to the simple
purchaser, who is not consoled to learn that
his loss is the gain of the next 'cute buyer, who
purchases at a figure under the real value of
the article, while a fair profit is enjoyed by
the vendor between the two extremes. How
patiently he undoes all his bundles, and lays
out the contents of his boxes, never retorting
a word to your angry dismissal! Although
amused the first day, and interested in seeing
his novel wares, I soon tired of the unceasing
interruption. One has hardly gone when
another succeeds him, and I took refuge in
pretending that I neither saw nor heard, while
the peddler tried first broken English, then
phrases of French, until I could not resist
laughing aloud. Arabs are sometimes seen
engaged in this line of business, but they are
not so patient or so politic. A Chinaman
always waits till his predecessor goes ere he

comes forward with his goods. An Arab was one morning spreading before me boxes of tortoise - shell and sandal - wood, embroidered slippers, jewellery, fans, muslins, &c., when another pushed forward, saying in the most laughable English, "Madam, do not buy from that man,—he tells lies, and he is a Mohammedan; I am Christian, and I will not cheat you." But his face belied him. The Arabs, too, do a little business in the town as shopkeepers and money-lenders, but in a much quieter and less obtrusive way than the Chinese. They are oftener owners of some sort of coasting craft, with which they trade from port to port, and to the outlying islands.

Some of the most elegant mansions in Batavia are owned by wealthy Chinese and Arabs; but strong restrictions are laid upon both nationalities because of their intriguing disposition, limiting even the number of horses that may be run in their carriages, while they are prohibited from trading in the interior of the island.

The Javanese do not perform the most menial work. They have an exceedingly refined cast of feature, are highly intelligent, have a different bearing and wear a different dress from the

B

Natives, as one calls the Sundanese and coast Malays. These natives are vehicle - drivers, small traders, and assistants to the Chinese, but the bulk of them are coolies. The more intelligent are household servants, but as a rule their intelligence is not of a high order, while they are very lazy and inclined to dishonesty.

## CHAPTER II.

JAVA, BUITENZORG——BOTANIC GARDEN——MORNING WALKS——
VISITS OF CEREMONY——SONG OF THE CICADS——MOSQUITOES
——LIFE IN THE TROPICS——A NATIVE FEAST——THE THEATRE
——DANCES——OUR ROUTE.

BUITENZORG.

WE are here established in the Hotel du Chemin de Fer, where the French host and hostess are very kind. Buitenzorg (the word means "freedom from care") is one of the chief holiday and health resorts of sick Batavians, and possesses not only a magnificent climate, but scenery of great beauty and picturesqueness. It is overlooked by two large and, at present, harmless volcanic mountains—the Salak, with its disrupted cone, into whose very heart one looks through the terrible cleft in its side ; and the double-peaked Pangerango and Gede, out of whose crater is ever lazily curling up white vapoury smoke from the simmering water which at present fills the summit of its pipe. Besides the fine views

to be had in its neighbourhood, Buitenzorg is
chiefly remarkable for its botanic garden, perhaps
the finest in the world, which surrounds the
Governor-General's unofficial residence. Every
morning finds us in these gardens. I have
already learnt that if you wish any enjoyment of
the tropical day you must be up before the sun,
and get out when his light is just coming over
the horizon. The freshness of this hour, when a
soft wind blows, bearing sweetest scents, almost
compensates for the great heat, which comes too
soon, and which the dusk does not relieve, for the
earth still sends off a heated air that makes the
wind warm. H. has been in Buitenzorg several
times; he knows the gardens well, and shows
me many beautiful details I might have passed
unnoticed. On the right, the garden descends
through groves and arbours, whose luxuriance of
growth and richness of leaf are new to my eye,
to its boundary stream, now (for it is the rainy
season) rushing and foaming over the great
boulders of rock which lie in its bed. Standing
on the terrace by its bank, under a canopy of
tall palms that form a shade from the early sun,
and looking over the torrent to stretches of fresh
green fields, we taste the sweetness of a tropical
morning. A beautiful vista towards the other

side of the town has recently been opened near
the palace, of which the photograph I send gives
only the faintest idea. The foreground has been
cleared by the felling of a wide strip of great
trees, and in their place is now a smooth lawn,
studded with plots of many varieties of flourish-
ing roses, from which the eye lifts itself to the
towering heights of the Salak mountain, whose
distant, bare, burnt sides are in strong contrast
to the verdure close at hand.

A long wide avenue of kanarie-trees, which
interlace high overhead in a superb leafy canopy,
traverses the garden ; and by the stream, another
of great banyan-trees forms a tunnel-like corridor.
On the left of the central walk are two others less
striking, but more remarkable. One is of Brazil-
ian palms, whose globular base and smooth-ringed
stems, straight and symmetrical, as if turned
in a lathe, contrast strongly in their whiteness
with the deep green of the leaf-sheaths and crown
of foliage; the other of bamboos, of various species
and most luxuriant growth. A slight breeze
generally rises about 10 A.M., and in the deep
shade of these avenues one can walk or drive at
noon in comfort. We never miss a daily visit to
a seat under an umbrageous India-rubber tree, in
front of which a fountain plays into a circular

pond, dotted with blue and white flowers of water-lilies and Victoria regias.

Occasionally we extend our morning walk to the environs, past the dwellings of the natives, whom we meet coming to market. If we stop a casual passer-by, and inquire the name for any tree, or flower, or bird, or insect that attracts us as we walk along, he can at once answer, explaining its use or habit. How neat their wares look in the deftly plaited case of strips of leaves or grass, or in a morsel of banana leaf, kept firm with a long thorn. How cleverly they utilise leaves, cocoa-nut shells, the bamboo, and other such products laid ready to their hand, as culinary utensils and tools for daily toil. Yes; nature is kind in this sunny land. One's heart need not ache for the starving, ill-clad, shelterless poor. Times of famine and waves of epidemic do occasionally distress the inhabitants, but these are rare. With sunshine, and comparative leisure to enjoy it, they are happy. It does one good to see the satisfied air of the humble natives, whose homes, though very poor, are not squalid or miserable.

All visits of ceremony are made in the evening, between sundown and 8 o'clock. It is customary to intimate in the morning your intention to call, and an answer is sent to let you know if your friends will be at home. A carriage costs the same for four hours as for one, and when you are going to call or to dine, it is ordered as soon as the declining sun makes it cool enough, and the fleet little steeds have taken you away out into the country before the short twilight ends. When your visit is over, they come back, flashing past the native houses, where fires for the evening meal burn red, and into the European neighbourhood, where guests are being received in brilliantly lighted verandahs.

When one does not wish to receive, the fore verandah is not so lighted. If at home, the family keep in the inner hall, or sit at one end of the verandah reading by a single lamp, or sway to and fro fanning themselves in the rocking-chairs, which are the chief furniture of all verandahs.

At the approach of dusk the ear is surprised by such a strange tumult that one eagerly asks, "What is it?" Is it the rush of distant water? Is it the noise from a thousand over-charged gas-burners? Is it the creaking of an overstrained mill, — that stridulous, rushing, whirring, buzzing sound, which rises and falls, and dies and swells again? It is only the song of the cicads, the bark of the frogs, the chirp of

the lizards—a sort of glee from the inhabitants
of the trees, bushes, and hedges.

Like all new-comers, I am tormented by mosquitoes. No precaution is absolute protection
from this pestering little foe. One wishes he
were more tangible, that he might be combated;
but so cleverly does he accomplish his cruel per-
secution that he is soaring off, buzzing his tri-
umph, before one begins to feel the tickling
which is but the precursor of days of irritation
from his little puncture. A lady advises me
never to retire without a candle (to search for
him), a towel (to slay him), and a bottle of eau
de Cologne (to allay his annoying wounds); but
despite such precautions he will sting the hand
raised to annihilate him, even while you are
watching for him to flit past. Death has been
known to ensue from a mosquito's bite. A
friend related to me that on first coming to
the Dutch Indies she all but lost her foot
through one. She was writing, and, intent on
her occupation, did not notice that she had
been scratching an inflamed bite with her shoe.
Shortly the foot commenced to swell, and soon
presented such an appearance as to cause her
great alarm. From this wound she was confined
to her sofa for a month, and it was for some

time under debate whether it would be necessary to amputate the foot. A gentleman who came on shore for the night in Batavia had his arm so swollen from two punctures that he was unable to dress next day, the inflammation being as severe as from vaccination. Mosquitoes are most annoying in the rainy season, for then they seek the shelter of the house; but always in the evening they buzz about near the lamp. Sometimes to read or write by lamplight is quite impossible. They do not allow one moment's peace; the only plan is to give yourself up to self-defence, and sit down with a fan and eyes on the alert. When the *salon* is arranged for the evening, shields are hung over the backs of the open canework chairs to prevent the mosquitoes stinging between the shoulders, where it is so difficult to relieve the tickling by rubbing.

Do I like life in the tropics? Yes, indeed, I am enchanted with all I see, I enjoy many indescribable sensations of delight—but do not envy me; you have compensating pleasures in England. When you walk among the scented pines, and the glinting sunbeams disclose in the modest seclusion of the tall grass the tiny starwort and the pretty veronica; when you go to meet the fresh wind blowing over a gorse-clad moor with step that

bounds to the lark's mad carolling overhead, know
that you have an enjoyment never to be had
here. Here is no joyous spring; here reigns
for ever an oppressiveness of richness, a mono-
tony of profusion, which cannot have the charm
of the sweet June-tide, the crown of the year.
There are no "sunless days when autumn leaves
wear a sunlight of their own," and you may never
see the fairy-like freaks of Father Frost.

I was fortunate enough, through the kindness
of our host of the hotel, to see a native feast,
given in honour of the son of the chief butler,
who had just finished his studies at school with
considerable credit. About 10 o'clock of a perfect moonlight night we set off for the scene of
the entertainment, some distance from the town,
and approached a greensward shut in by tall
trees, through arches festooned with greenery and
gay decorations of flowers. In the open air, in this
natural enclosure, the tables were already spread.
Preparations, we were told, had been in progress
for over a month, and the quantity of substantial
viands and confections of attractive colour and
skilful composition showed that the time must
have been busily employed. We found the
guests already seated, talking and gazing at
the tiers of plates containing the eatables,—for

it is only after hours of patient restraint that
the feasting commences on a signal being given.
Several hundreds occupied the tables arranged
for the general company; at a little distance,
almost curtained in by draperies of flowers and
foliage, by a white-covered table sat natives of
rank and importance in gay costumes and glittering jewels, relieved by the black coats of a few
European gentlemen.  We did not mean to partake, so were led to a canopied and carpeted dais,
where, however, we had set before us some of
the daintiest of the confections.  Beyond the
invited guests were hundreds more of onlookers,
who feast in their own way, purchasing from the
many vendors mingling in the crowd.  All, however, enjoy alike the theatre and the dance.  The
former is a ludicrous exhibition of a series of
grotesque hobgoblin creatures, which are represented on a large sheet by a magic lantern.
The advent of each fresh figure is greeted by
the beholders with screams of delight, which sink
into murmurs of criticism till the next moves
on the scene.

The dance is the performance of a youth and
a maiden, in which, however, the latter takes
the more prominent part.  Her hair was very
neatly arranged, and decked with white flowers.

She was gaily attired in a *sarong* of spangled purple velvet, and a bodice, compressing her shoulders like a vice, of the same. Over the purple skirt was another of green satin, edged with gold fringe ; and she not ungracefully manipulated an embroidered sash, casting it now over her shoulder, again round her wrists, as she contorted the hands and arms into attitudes outvying the achievements of a *danseuse.* The part played by the feet is very insignificant,— simply a gentle shuffling motion from the one to the other. At intervals the youth shuffled towards her from the edge of the circle, and after much preamble embraced her, wearing a countenance as expressionless as her own ; but this climax calls forth loud applause, which is responded to by a silly grin.

The monotonous clanging and tinkling of a native band suit well the slow movements of the dance. The chief instrument is the *gamelau,* consisting of a series of eight or ten gongs graduated in size, set in a bamboo frame, and played on much as the harmonica is, but with two sticks. We are told that in the hands of a skilful player very pleasing music is produced. A thinner sound is emitted from a similar series of anvil-looking blocks of metal, and these instruments

are supported by numerous flutes and primitive
two-stringed violins, as well as by cymbals and
tinkling instruments.  Through all booms the
deep note of a large single gong, set in a tripod
frame, the whole forming a massive if not over-
musical orchestra.  Each member of it seemed
to play with heart and soul, making ludicrous
facial contortions and genuflections, and swaying the body to and fro, as if carried away by
the enchantment of the music he produced.

We take passage on the 15th of this month
from Batavia to Amboina.  You remember our
destination is Timor-laut or Tenimber Islands,
a small group shown on the map as lying between the considerable islands of Papua or New
Guinea and Timor.  We shall get as far as
Amboina, in the Moluccas, by the Netherland
India steamer Bromo, and find other means of
proceeding thence to Timor-laut.  A steamer of
this company makes the tour of the archipelago
once a month, going from Macassar northwards,
coasting Celebes, calling at Amboina and Timor,
and passing through the Flores Straits to Macassar, one journey, and reversing the route the
next.  We happen to go by the southern route.
I shall do my best to post some news of our
progress at Macassar.

# CHAPTER III.

AT SEA—DUTCH OFFICIAL MIGRATIONS—SAMARANG—STRAITS OF MEDNEA — SURABAYA — MERMEN AND MERMAIDS— CARGO OF BIRDS — CHARACTERISTICS OF JAVA — THE DUTCH COLONIAL SYSTEM.

MACASSAR SEA.

WITH daylight on the 15th April we were speeding from the Hotel der Nederlanden, in Batavia, to the wharf, to embark in the steam-tender waiting to take us out to the roads, where the Bromo was riding at anchor. We had dined the previous evening in the suburbs, and afterwards attended a fancy-dress ball in the public gardens, returning after midnight to finish packing and make ready for the start early next morning. After this night of fatigue, the rapid drive in the cool morning air was delightfully refreshing, and I wished it could have lasted some hours instead of thirty minutes. The sun rose too quickly, and waiting on the steam-tender till all was ready was indeed trying. Officers looked overburdened in their cumbersome uniforms, and ladies seemed distressed in European clothing. One lady fainted, and every one suffered until we set off and caught the breeze from the sea : when we had climbed to the deck of the Bromo it was comparatively cool.

The bulk of the passengers by this route are officials changing residence from one part to another of the Dutch possessions, or military officers changing their station. We learn that when such a change is ordered, the furniture of the old home is sold, because transport is so very dear. With the proceeds of the sale all debts are paid, and a fresh start is made. But in some remote parts furniture could not be purchased, and all that is needful must be taken. All have some household gods to which they cling : there are flowers, and the children's domestic pets cannot be left behind, so the ship is like a garden and menagerie combined, while furniture not only crowds the deck, but is hung in every available space overhead, so low that one must always be looking out to avoid being bumped.

We are a considerable company, a floating village. Besides the saloon passengers on our deck, there are the maid and men servants, who

are in constant attendance on the families with
whom they are going to the new home. There
is no defined place for these *boys* and *baboos :*
they sleep on the floor of the saloon, without
pillow or mat, wearing the dress of the day-
time. Going down in the dim lamplight, one
has to be careful to avoid falling over some
dusky slumbering form ; and despite the utmost
heedfulness, an arm or foot extended by the
unconscious sleeper trips you up, and sends you
stumbling on to the head of another.

The cabins receive no attention from the ship
servants, and one who has not learnt this arrangement suffers considerable discomfort, for no per-
suasion avails to induce them to keep one's cabin
clean and in order. This seems equally strange
to another party on board, the family of the
governor-elect of Portuguese Timor, who are
on their way from Portugal. The ladies of this
party are the only Europeans who, like myself,
wear European dress. We had not been half
an hour on deck when the Dutch ladies appeared in *sarong* and *kabia,* looking greatly
relieved in the light clothing. Common-sense
must admit that, for suitability to the climate,
no dress can compare with it. How very different the scene is from that on an English

steamer! I find endless amusement in simply looking on.

In two days we moored off Samarang, having seldom lost sight of the much-indented coast of Java, which presented to our view ranges of undulating hills, backed by imposing mountains. The shallowness of the harbour of Samarang does not admit of anchorage within several miles from the mouth of the canal, which, as at Batavia, leads to the town. Being still fatigued from the exertions of the days preceding our departure, we did not attempt to go on shore. The heat was insufferable as we lay these two days motionless in the bay, and it was the greatest relief to start for the next port, Surabaya, where it is required that all disembark with their whole possessions for five days. Sailing straight to Amboina, without any stoppage, would take about one week. The expense of a voyage, and the loss of time, are considerable when you must go all round the archipelago, and wait at different ports until the vessel is ready to proceed. But there is absolutely no other means of travel : this company has a monopoly, and voyagers have no alternative except the risks and dangers of a native prahu, to face which the experience of another traveller did not invite us. Mr Wallace

C

spent thirty - eight days on a voyage which
should have been accomplished in twelve, and
had to struggle constantly against wind and
tide.

We passed through the Straits of Mednea in
the night, and early in the morning of the 19th
April were in the bustle of disembarking for the
five days, until the steamer should resume its
voyage. There is the same level foreshore as at
Batavia and Samarang, and the same manner of
approaching by a long canal. The row from the
ship to the canal was over before the heat of the
day commenced, and we were ready to be towed
along from the custom-house by eight o'clock.
Men tow on each bank by long ropes, and manage
very cleverly to keep clear of the barges and
boats of all kinds which crowd the canal. Some
ships and tenders of considerable size passed us,
and the gay dresses of the crews, and the bright-
painted vessels, made this canal scene a most
animated picture. We landed at our hotel simultaneously with the Da França family, having
kept up from our several boats a conversation on
the novel sight passing us. We gained its
shelter with some thankfulness, after our long
exposure to the sun.

The hotel resembles greatly in construction the

one in which we lived in Batavia : our room this time, however, is in the front part of the buildding. I am now accustomed to hotel life in Java, and amuse myself at my ease, looking on the busy scene. The same round goes on, the early rising, the busy morning, the ample lunch, the afternoon of rest, and the gay evening. How refreshing it is to go driving at the sunset hour with those sharp-trotting ponies. If you wish to go beyond the town any considerable distance, it is the rule to drive with four horses. One such excursion we had occasion to take, and as the scenery of the environs of Surabaya is exceedingly pretty, we had no slight pleasure in the drive.

The town is of no mean size, and is a busy seat of trade : its importance is added to by a large dock, where ships from all parts are repaired. There is, besides, a Government arsenal, and these industries bring a considerable European population. Their pleasant homes are in a suburb which we had occasion several times to visit, to enjoy the hospitality of kind friends. Public gardens laid out with much taste are a great amenity, and it is customary to descend for half an hour in the course of the evening drive to walk in the shrubberies and hear the excellent music of the band.

Entering a Chinaman's shop in the crowded part of the town to make some purchases, we saw a wonderful collection of curiosities. Among these were some carved statues of great value and interest, but most curious to us were a mummified merman and mermaid. These I had always thought to be fabulous creations of simple-minded seafarers, but those we saw were certainly sufficient to give origin to the tales we have heard of them. The upper part of the body is quite human in form, and is smooth-skinned; the face is ape-like, but human enough to suggest the comparison, only there is no hair on the head. The fore-limbs are arms with five fingers. The lower part of the body is that of a fish with scales and fins.

We saw also a cargo of birds just arrived from New Guinea, and ready for despatch to Europe —2000 skins of the orange-feathered bird of paradise, 800 of the king-bird, and a various lot of others. This, remember, was only one cargo, and the traffic will go on the whole season. Such a fearful slaughter of these lovely birds is really distressing. Soon we shall have lost off the face of the globe these unique and most gorgeous of the feathered tribes. There were also some skins of the rare six-shafted or golden paradise bird. It is figured by Mr Wallace in his 'Malay Archipelago,' but the illustration gives no idea of its velvety plumage.

Surabaya is low-lying and sultry, but the heat at mid-day is not by any means so trying as on shipboard. The early mornings at sea are delightfully fresh, and with the sunset hour comes a welcome wind, while the evening is cool : the afternoon, however, is almost unendurable, especially when lying still in harbour. The double awnings are baked, the decks are hot, the glistening sea reflects pitilessly the powerful sun, giving no relief to the tired eyes, and sending up only an air as from an oven : nowhere is there any escaping from the strong heat. Here, in a dwelling constructed for coolness, it is by no means unbearable. Sometimes, seated in a shady verandah, listlessly rocking to and fro, one is lulled into dreams of home, and visions flit through the mind of winter evenings and blazing hearths, and the comfort of listening to the fierce wind whistling in the gables ; and, involuntarily, comparisons will intrude of the respective merits of chilblains and prickly heat.

Our next port is Macassar, which we reach after a sail of two days and two nights. We

leave behind us the most beautiful, as well as
the most fertile, most productive, and most
populous tropical island in the world, of which
I regret that I am able to say so little, for I
have scarcely more than coasted it. Java is
magnificently varied with mountain and forest
scenery, and is by no means inaccessible to the
tourist. The famous Daendals, while Governor-
General of the Dutch Indies from 1808 to 1811,
caused roads to be made that even now excite
the admiration of every visitor. Important
railway routes have been opened up within the
last two years; but in many districts posting is
still necessary, a mode of travelling which the
nature of the country renders full of excitement
and danger. I have good authority for stating
that no post-horses in Europe can compare with
those of Java.

Let me quote a few sentences for your information :—

"This island possesses many mountains, some
rising ten or twelve thousand feet high; the
abundant moisture and tropical heat of the
climate causes them to be clothed with luxuriant vegetation often to their very summit,
while forests and plantations cover their lower
slopes. The animal productions, especially the

birds and insects, are beautiful and varied, and present many peculiar forms found nowhere else upon the globe. The soil throughout the island is exceedingly fertile, and all the productions of the tropics, together with many of the temperate zones, can be easily cultivated. Java, too, possesses a civilisation, a history, and antiquities of its own, of great interest. The Brahminical religion flourished in it from an epoch of unknown antiquity till about the year 1478, when that of Mahomet superseded it. The former religion was accompanied by a civilisation which has not been equalled by the conquerors; for, scattered through the country, especially in the eastern parts of it, are found buried in lofty forests, temples, tombs, and statues of great beauty and grandeur, and the remains of extensive cities, where the tiger, the rhinoceros, and the wild bull now roam undisturbed."

"To the ordinary English traveller, the Malay Archipelago is perhaps the least known part of the earth. Few persons realise that as a whole it is comparable with the primary divisions of the globe, and that some of its separate islands are larger than France or the Austrian Empire. The traveller soon, however, acquires different ideas. He comes to look upon this region as one apart from the rest of the world, with its own races of men and its own aspects of nature; with its own ideas, feelings, customs, and modes of speech, and with a climate, vegetation, and animated life altogether peculiar to itself."

Although I had read that this archipelago contains three islands larger than Great Britain, and that it would stretch over an expanse equal to that of all Europe from the extreme west far into Central Asia, the associations of my childhood have so chained my mind, that till now I have been unable to dissever the tiny specks depicted on the map between Asia and Australia from their Liliputian proportions.

Holland adopts a different system from our own in her subject possessions. She accommodates herself to the natives, conducting intercourse of all kinds in their language. The construction of the Malay tongue is most simple, and I find it exceedingly pleasant to the ear; there are, besides, no impossible sounds. I have seldom heard the Javanese language; it is much more difficult to acquire, but has a more elegant and refined sound.

We are now nearing Macassar. The Da França family are our constant companions. H. speaks a little Portuguese, while they all speak French as fluently as their own tongue. They are a party of fourteen,—Monsieur and Madame, their eldest son and his wife, two young ladies, and six young children. Their good *bonne*, old Jacinthe, is the thirteenth, and accompanying them is Monsieur Fontes, a naval officer going to command the Government vessel which rides in the Bay of Timor.

# CHAPTER IV.

*Coasting* FLORES, 30*th April.*

IT has been very rough and almost cold crossing
from Macassar to Sumbawa, and we were truly
thankful to gain the shelter of the Bay of Bima.
When you are fairly in, no outlet can be seen,
and the general aspect of the bay with its
mountainous surroundings vividly suggests Loch
Lomond. A few short hours, and we were out
again on the troubled waters. To-day, however,
we are running along the coast of Flores, the
Land of Flowers of the early Portuguese
mariners, in more placid waters, and I make
an attempt to continue.

We lay four days at Macassar, and had ample
opportunity to see all that is to be seen. Let

me first say that I saw no Macassar oil. I
looked in every window, and read every sign-
board, and scanned every building that might
be a factory, and asked every one I came in
contact with, but no one knew anything about
Macassar oil!

Macassar is the point from which the products
of Western civilisation are disseminated through
the barbarous East, and is one of the great em-
poriums of the native trade of the archipelago.
Rattans from Borneo, sandal-wood and bee's-wax
from Flores and Timor, tripang from the Gulf
of Carpentaria, cajeput-oil from Bouru, wild
nutmegs and mussoi-bark from New Guinea,—
are all to be found in the stores of the Chinese
and Bugis merchants of Macassar, along with
the rice and coffee which are the chief products
of the surrounding country. There is also the
trade to the Aru Islands, of which almost the
whole produce comes to Macassar in native
vessels to contribute to the luxurious tastes of
the most civilised races. Pearls, mother-of-
pearl, and tortoise-shell find their way to
Europe, while edible birds'-nests and tripang,
or sea-slug, are sent off by ship-loads for the
gastronomic enjoyment of the Chinese.

Near the wharf Macassar has quite a business

aspect. Here for the first time we had the comfort of being moored to the shore; by simply
crossing the gangway we were on *terra firma.*
Passing from the wharf, one enters a long street
where European, Chinese, and Arab warehouses
and shops are closely wedged; it opens into a
broad avenue of stately trees which skirt a green
sward. The grounds of the Government mansions open from the avenue, and here also are
the best European houses, with a good club-
house or reading-room, where the 'Graphic' and
many good papers may be seen. An imposing
fort, very white against the grass, fills one end
of the green. I like walking when possible, one
gets so cramped on board ship, so each morning
we made our way to the outskirts, passing frequently through some native village. In one of
these I first tasted the milk of the cocoa-nut,
and saw the expert way of obtaining the nuts
from the tall trees. Slight notches are cut all
up the stem at the distance of a stride, by which
with unfaltering steps the gatherer mounts, plac-
ing the great toe in the notches. A cocoa-nut
tree is exceedingly beautiful; the long, smooth,
upright grey stem is just fit to be crowned with
the feathery plumes that bend so gracefully over
it. The nut gathered fresh is very different from

the fruit as seen sold in our markets.  The colourless liquid which issues on the nut being opened
has the appearance of water, but has a slightly
sweet flavour, and is most refreshing.  The
natives allowed us to enter their dwellings,
and seemed as pleased to have a white visitor
as she was to make herself acquainted with the
interior of a bamboo-hut.

In one long street edging the beach there is a
series of miniature shipbuilding yards, where the
famous Macassar prahus are built.  These vessels
are of such curious construction that a short description might interest you.  Looking at a
native prahu, you would scarcely care to trust
yourself to a voyage of some thousands of miles
in it, but they cruise all over the archipelago
with as few casualties as any other sort of
craft.  The shape suggests a Chinese junk.
Some are as small as a fishing-coble—I speak of
one of about eighty tons burden, with about
thirty of a crew.  The deck slopes greatly down
to the bows : it is thus the lowest part of the
vessel which cuts the waves.  The strangest part
of its construction, and a source of much appre-
hension to any called to trust their life in a
prahu for a considerable voyage, is a large hole
about a yard square which runs through the

after-part of the vessel three feet above the water line, and which is actually open to the hold. It is quite puzzling how these boats weather a storm without being swamped by the first half-dozen seas.

The fittings and appliances are all of native material, and there is an absence of the qualmish smells incident to a steamer,—" no grease, no oil, no varnish; instead of these, bamboo, rattan, and palm thatch, all pure vegetable fibres, which, if they smell at all, smell pleasantly, and recall quiet scenes in the green and shady forest." Mr Wallace says of a twenty days' voyage in one, that he never travelled with so little discomfort, and this he attributes to the absence of paint, pitch, tallow, and new cordage, to the freedom from all restraint of meal hours and of dress. This last consideration is by no means insignificant. It is often simply a trial to the flesh to sit out dinner in the saloon of a steamer in the usual dress. The large company in the limited space, the many servants, the smoking dishes, create a temperature which, long ere the tedious meal is finished, induces a streaming perspiration, and one leaves the table with garments almost as wet as if one had been bathing instead of dining in them. Still, if one is anxious to reach a destination in a given time, the steam-vessel has doubtless the advantage over a Macassar prahu.

Numbers of these prahus, as well as many steamers and sailing-vessels of varied build, with the large white guard-ship, make the Macassar roadstead gay and animated ; and although to us, leaving behind the busier centres, it seems the first taste of rusticity, I can imagine that on a return from the seclusion of the isles around, it must seem the gate of life. In Macassar resides one of the three governors that are under the Governor - General of the Dutch Indies. The position of these is kept up with some dignity. Visits were exchanged between the Governors of Timor and Macassar, and the latter's carriage, with four fleet cream-coloured ponies, was morning and evening at the Da França family's disposal.

I had the first touch of fever I have experienced just after leaving Macassar : probably I had been out in the sun too much. It was not severe,—just sufficient to produce an unconquerable lassitude. Lying on a sofa one evening at dusk, apparently asleep, when all the others were down dressing for dinner, I heard a continual talking near by me : gently turning, I saw one of the governor's little lads seated within a circle of chairs, stools, and footstools. In childish fashion he was holding over again the reception which his father had that afternoon given to the Governor of Macassar and suite, and with bows and compliments and the most gracious manner was conversing with the imaginary circle of visitors. I was intensely amused, and dared not move lest I should discomfit the boy by the discovery that he was observed.

This voyage gives an excellent opportunity of seeing the relations of the Dutch with their native servants. These, both male and female, loll or crouch about the deck all day, ready to run down-stairs on an errand for the mistress or children, or bring a light for master's cigar. Children all speak Malay, and repeat their little tales and rhymes in that language. Their Dutch speech until they go to school is very imperfect.

At Larantuka, before entering the strait of that name, some of the gentlemen went on shore to visit a Catholic settlement : it was then raining so heavily that we could not accompany them. The wooded slopes, as we approached the village, seemed to invite nestling villas and turreted chateaux, while the tiny spire of the chapel looked a promise of peaceful safety. But there is a reason for the closely crowded monastery buildings and the strong stockade which we could see encircling them. The natives, except the villagers who have come under the civilising influence of the priests, live in the mountains, and every now and again come down and make a night-raid on the establishment, in such force that they always have the best of the fray.

The priests were evidently glad to have European visitors, and treated our party with every kindness. H. bought a pair of shell armlets, which were with the utmost difficulty withdrawn from the wearer's arm ; another tried to get hers off, but it was found impossible. These ornaments are put on in childhood, and as the person grows they form a groove in the arm, from which it is surprising that strangulation of the limb does not ensue.

*Crossing the* BANDA SEA.

We were in Cupang, the capital of the Dutch half of the island of Timor, the day after our passage through the beautiful Flores Straits. As soon as our anchor dropped in the bay, we were surrounded by small boats, whose rowers had quite a distinctive appearance, arising from

D

their dressy attire, which, however, is simple
enough when examined. On their shoulders
they wear a fringed plaid hanging in the graceful fashion of the Highland costume. Their
hats—such wonderful hats !—are made of the
pale spathe of the Borassus palm-tree, and besides the neatly constructed crown and "Devon-
shire" brim, they are elaborately ornamented
with a mass of flowers and plumes, wonderfully
modelled from chips of the spathe. Such a hat
would be most becoming to a fair English girl;
but to these male wearers, with their sooty
skins and wild frizzly mops, they gave the
most grotesque appearance.

On going on shore we were delighted to find
there an Englishman, who took us to his home
and left us to the good care of his wife and
daughter, by whose hospitable kindness we enjoyed a pleasant change from shipboard, and
had the opportunity of seeing and learning a
deal of life in Cupang. The ladies insisted that
I should get off my English clothing and try
the comfort of the *sarong* and *kabia*. Mrs
Drysdale informs me that every Dutch lady
takes pride in her store of these garments, and
a dozen dozens of the jacket is not considered
an over-stock. She showed me beautiful ex-

amples of the skirt, some almost cloth-of-gold from the quantity of it inwoven, while others were curious specimens of patterns of native fancy. I saw for the first time a fashion of belt worn by some to support the skirt instead of the usual sash : it is of pure beaten gold of native workmanship, richly chased all round, though only the clasp is ever seen on a chance opening of the jacket. There was also one of silver, less elaborate. These belts are highly valued, and handed down as heir-looms. I also learnt that there is considerable art in the proper arrangement of the *sarong*. On each of the poorest as well as of the richest make there is a strip called the *kapala*, which must fall straight down the left leg just on the top of the fold containing the fulness. It is part of the costume to wear a medallion or pretty ornament on a necklace amongst the lace of the neck of the *kabia*, which is made slightly open for the purpose, while jewelled studs are worn to fasten it instead of buttons.

As soon as it was cool enough we walked out, and found Cupang a bright, clean, neatly laid-out town, situated at the base of abrupt hills. It has a considerable Dutch population, living in pretty substantial houses, embowered in

greenery. The true natives of Timor we did
not see : they come down from their mountain
homes only occasionally to meet purchasers of
bee's-wax, dammar for torches, and such products ; but no intercourse can be established, for
they will not conform to civilisation. Trade is
conducted by barter, tobacco being a favourite
article of exchange ; but they will strive for years
to get the means of purchasing a species of bead
of a reddish colour, evidently a sort of soft
stone, giving for it more than its weight in
gold. Whence these beads come is quite unknown ; the natives say they are pulled off the
grass blades in certain spots *very* early in the
morning. The counterfeit beads made in Bir-
mingham for the Chinese traders are excellent
imitations, but the native is not to be deceived
into giving the price of the genuine article.
A complete string of eight or nine inches costs
about £12.

Trade in Cupang is in the hands chiefly of
Chinese and Arabs : the dark race we met in
the streets are natives of the island of Solor,
who are imported for servants and coolies.

From Macassar to Cupang we had a Chinese
gentleman as saloon passenger, and as I had
never before occasion to be so near a member

of the Celestial Empire, I took the opportunity
to study his *tout ensemble*. How does it come
that John Chinaman has a rich development
of unusual length, where John Bull has only a
shining bare patch? One afternoon when H.
was talking to our Chinese companion, I
seated myself close behind and examined his
distinctive feature. Every bit of the head is
clean shaved except this patch on the crown,
which, thick enough itself, is reinforced by a
quantity of red silk, which is interwoven with
it, and forms a fringe at the point. Our friend's
white calico jackets and spacious trousers were
specimens of perfect laundry-work, while the
loose coats of cloth or silk which he wore in
the cooler hours were beautifully tailored, and
ornamented with jewelled buttons set in gold.
As we were walking through the town, he hailed
us from his door, and invited us in to have tea.
His little sons, evidently in holiday attire to
celebrate their father's return home, served us
with the pale liquid as they drink it, without
sugar or cream; his ladies did not appear further
than to stand peeping round a screen. His
house was handsomely furnished in Chinese
style, with numerous pagodas and cabinets and
much gilding. Surely home is as dear to a

Chinaman as to an Englishman : this good man
sustained the part of master of the house with
evident pride, and seemed complacently happy
on his return to the familiar surroundings.

The poor class of Chinese wear blue trousers,
white being reserved for the rich. But all
alike have the white jacket, which is always
clean and fresh, for the Chinese are prized as
laundry-workers all over the East. Some have
white silk inwoven in the pig-tail, the elderly
substituting black, for thus the growing scanti-
ness of age is not so apparent. Even an old
man of eighty has a creditable plait, and the
pride of all wearers is evinced by the frequency
with which the appendage is drawn round and
gazed at, and felt and stroked.

There is in Cupang a large Chinese and Arab
population, and I could not help contrasting the
two races. The Chinaman everywhere has a
bright, clean, active look : he moves with a
briskness refreshing to see in that land of loitering, and always seems on business intent. The
Arab, again, is all folds and twists. His dress has
undoubtedly the more picturesque appearance.
His loose flowing apparel of various colours,
richly embroidered vest, jacket, and gay turban,
attract the eyes far off : you watch him approach

with majestic carriage, until he is before you
with his noble features, soft dark eyes, and
curling locks. You find him much bejewelled,
generally with paltry rings and chains, though
the rich often possess very valuable ones.

A heavy shower in the afternoon gave us
the opportunity of seeing the natives use their
primitive umbrella, a single leaf of lontar palm,
which forms an excellent shelter. They rush
along, crouching under the leaf as if they had
plumes and satins to spoil.

A lovely moonlight night succeeded, and being
joined by the Da França family from the ship,
we walked together to the outskirts to examine
the elaborate tombs which stud the slopes round
the town, erected within no defined graveyard,
but on any spot chosen by the owners.

This was our last evening together. Next
forenoon we were at Dilly, their destination, the
capital of Portuguese territory in the eastern
half of the island. We parted with deep regret
from our courteous and accomplished companions; but with the hope that it will at some
future time be possible to avail ourselves of
their cordial invitation to visit Timor, his Excellency having offered every aid in his power
should H. wish to travel in the interior.

"Little Madame," as we call her, to distinguish
her from her stately mother-in-law, and Mademoiselle Isabel have been my principal companions, but we have all been much together,
and have so enjoyed our intercourse that it
seems as if there could be no more pleasure in
the rest of the voyage.

They landed under a salute from the fort,
with a great show of ceremony ; and after the
governor had received the keys of office in the
church, we joined them at lunch and saw them
installed in their new home. The palace has
an imposing enough aspect from the bay, but on
a nearer approach it is seen to be rather dilapidated, and I grieve for their sakes to learn that
Dilly is most unhealthy. The supreme evil of
the town is that it is built on a low morass,
causing incessant fever, which robs the inhabitants of all energy, and explains at once the
rather miserable aspect of this compared with
other towns of similar size.

Quantities of large red-painted cases were dis-
charged from our vessel and piled on the shore
here, as at every other port we had called at.
These contain bottles filled with a coarse fiery gin,
which is used greatly in barter with the natives
by traders, and is only too eagerly accepted.

# CHAPTER V.

*6th May.*

THERE had been much talk during the voyage of
the islands of Banda, the chief nutmeg-garden
of the world, and we were naturally curious to
see them for ourselves.

Banda is the most lovely spot we have yet
visited. Coming on deck early, we found ourselves approaching a dense and brilliant vegetation, in strong contrast to the bare spurs of
Timor, which we had left a few days before.
Steaming in through a narrow winding entrance, which seemed after giving us passage
to glide together, we found ourselves in a deep-
blue inland lake. But only apparently. The
Banda group is composed of four small islands,
three of which form this secure harbour. Three
of the four are covered over almost their entire

surface with nutmeg-trees. As though to form
an offset to this luxuriance and fertility, towers
the terrible fire-mountain Gunung Api, which
reeks eternally from its shapely cone, like a
fierce guardian of these gardens of Paradise.
A sulphureous smoke ever rises from its bare
and scarred summit, but its base and flanks
are green with trees, amid whose shade a white
dwelling here and there peeps out, heedless of
the internal fires that blister the smouldering
cone. How strange it was to lean on the ship's
rail, and gaze down into the tranquil harbour,
whose waters are so transparent that living
corals, and even the minutest objects, are
plainly seen on the volcanic sand at a depth of
seven or eight fathoms; then to lift the eyes to
the smoking mountain, and picture the terrible
tumult in the fiery caverns within !

Passing from the shore, along which runs a
row of clean-looking whitewashed houses, the
steep shady path to the left leads to the
gardens; keeping to the right, you ascend to
the town. Following one street and then
another, having on each side Arab, Chinese,
and Malay shops, where all necessities, such as
food, clothing, and coffins, are displayed for
purchase, you emerge on a green level bordered

by some good houses and a church. On the
sward is the village well, where there seems
always to be a group of busy washers; and in
the centre is a large school, where every edu-
cational advantage may be enjoyed, so that
European residents need not, as formerly, send
their children to distant parts to be educated.
On its left rises the battlemented fort built
by the Portuguese, but now flying the Dutch
ensign, from the top of which a magnificent
view is to be had of the surrounding islands
and out over the boundless sea. Sitting on
the topmost of a long flight of steps, we looked
down on the Banda isles, so small in their vast
setting,—on the volcano, from whose crest the
vapour - cloud had temporarily lifted, leaving
the whole symmetrical outline clearly defined,
—on the reposeful town, heedless of the terrible
devastation which has overwhelmed, and at any
moment may again overwhelm it from the over-
shadowing fire-mountain,—on the land-locked
bay, bathed in sunlight and gently ruffled by
the breeze, which floated out the flags on the
shipping, — and down on the old fort, which
tells how the spice-gardens of Insulinde were
valued in other centuries.

We called each day of our stay at Bin Saleh's,

an Arab, whose cases of paradise and other gay
birds' skins from New Guinea and other islands
of the archipelago, ready for despatch to the
Paris markets, were a great attraction.  He invited us into his inner room, where he showed
us a small bunch of tortoise-shell, for which he
said he could readily get £50 in Singapore.  In
his back-court is an Arab school, and I was
allowed to look in on the company of little
fellows, who were squatted round their teacher,
and whose sing-song, simultaneous repetition of
their lesson resounded through the neighbourhood.

Starting with the sun one morning, we climbed
the slope to the left by a path overhung with
gracefully bending bamboos and overgrown with
lycopods, which leads into the nutmeg woods.
The nutmeg-trees are rather sparsely planted,
and form a thin grove under a canopy of tall
kanarie-trees, which interlace high overhead.
The paths through the woods are as wide as a
carriage-way, and well made.  Tired of the ship,
we wandered on for miles, till we came to one
of the plantation houses, a small village of buildings, where men, women, and children were employed preparing the nuts and mace for export.
Neither of these products is at all like what we

see at home, the rich colours being quite lost in drying. Now and then we met a gatherer, a picturesque object in his bright clothing among the green foliage. With a pole jointed like a fishing-rod he nips the stalk of the ripe nuts by two claw-like prongs with which the tip of his rod is armed, when they drop into a little basket-like cage worked to the stem some inches below. We stopped him to look at his creel full of the ripe fruit. The shining chestnut-brown nut, broidered with the deep scarlet mace, nestles in the half - open pale yellow shell, and is indeed a thing of beauty. The nutmeg is the favourite food of the large pigeons we heard booming their note in the quiet woods. These pigeons are frequently seen tame about homesteads, and are very pretty creatures. They are rather larger than a guinea-fowl, but not so large as a pea-hen, while the shape is quite that of a pigeon. The plumage is a deep slate grey, with a tinge towards bluish-purple, and a tuft of fine delicate feathers gives it its name of crown pigeon.

By the shore, just on the wharf, are the depots from which the fruits and mace are despatched, with wood-yards where the packing-cases are made. The cases are all of one size,

and are carefully finished and caulked. The
produce of the nutmeg-tree forms as cleanly
an article of cargo as could be wished. A box
measuring about three feet by two by one contains £20 worth of nutmegs, and such a box
will hold from £30 to £40 worth of mace.

We are now steaming straight for Amboina,
where this stage of our journey to the Tenimber
Islands ends. I am now quite familiar with the
manner of life on shipboard. I take full advantage of the privilege, denied to ladies on English
vessels, of appearing on deck before certain
hours. Here all come up with daylight, all
equally in *negligé* costume, to enjoy the freshness of the morning wind. Coffee is offered
as soon as one appears on deck. Breakfast,
with cold meat and eggs, is on the saloon table
for several hours after 7, and one descends to
partake or has it brought on deck at will.
About 10, soup with toast is offered, or if the
day is intensely hot, some liqueur with effer-
vescent water. About 12, the advent of a stand
with gin and bitters, vermuth and sherry, an-
nounces that lunch will be served in half an
hour, and it is the habit of most Dutch gentlemen to whet the appetite with the first of these,
while vermuth is taken by the ladies as a tonic.

Lunch consists of the "rice table," such as I described when writing from Batavia; then about 3, when people begin to rise from the sofas on deck, and emerge from cabins after the siesta, tea is ready. When the afternoon heat has sufficiently passed to make it possible, all go down to dress in European attire. When we return to deck, the beautiful sunset hour has come with a cool breeze, and it is customary to walk to and fro on the deck till the liqueur-stand reminds us that we must soon go down to dine. After dinner at 7.30, the European dress is quickly discarded, and all seek retired nooks on the dimly lighted deck to enjoy the evening wind. You can have no idea of the lassitude felt at the close of a day on shipboard in the tropics. One gets very disinclined for exercise towards the end of a protracted voyage, and it becomes more and more difficult to occupy one's self in any way. I sometimes wish I had not promised to take you with me in my travels !

I forget if I told you that children of both sexes play all day in a sort of very loose "combination," of striped calico generally, their sole garment,—for not even shoes and stockings do they wear. But one cannot grudge them the comfort of this simple costume : think how quickly it is put on, how readily changed, how easily washed. A Dutch lady on board tells me that when a journey is contemplated, friends and neighbours lend linen both for personal and for household use for some time before departure, and so the traveller has the advantage of starting with everything clean.

I have learnt that any kind of clothing containing dye is objectionable, and also that for us, who are constantly travelling, quantities of linen clothing are a nuisance. It accumulates in the cabin for one thing, and when one comes to port and gives it out to be hastily washed, the destruction of all finer things is heart-breaking, while every button is sacrificed. Besides, the starch used is either sour or gets so in the moist climate, and the clothes have a most unpleasant odour if shut up for any time in a box. It seems to me that clothing of pure undyed wool is most suitable. If you contemplate travel in the tropics, I should recommend you to study Dr Jaeger's 'Woollen System.' I should also recommend you to try to get a good native or, better, Chinese maid. A European would be of no use, besides that there is no proper accommodation either in hotels or on steamers for white servants.

*May 7th.*

We are now steaming into the Bay of Amboina; the scenery is very beautiful, but I am too anxious to speak of that at present. We go straight to visit the Resident on landing, and hope for a kind reception. A Resident is, as it were, a sub-governor, but in this remote part—nearly a month by mail from the capital of the archipelago—he is practically an autocrat, and our success really now depends upon his goodwill. But why should we fear? We have every reason to expect his co-operation, and indeed every right, for H. bears the warmest recommendations from the Government. Besides, the Dutch are proverbially hospitable; and H. has enjoyed such kindness during all his travels, that we may look for a continuance of it now.

E

# CHAPTER VI.

*AMBOINA, 12th May.*

SUPPOSE you were to undertake a long journey with some special and laudable object, and were furnished with hearty recommendations to the lord of the place of your destination, who alone could further your work; suppose yourself landed there, and seated with high hope in the gentleman's presence, talking of all sorts of subjects, hearing of the capabilities of the land and of his excellent opportunities of acquainting himself therewith, while he shows you the treasures he has collected. You have presented your introductions, you expect that in time conversation will turn to your errand, and that the aid you looked for will be readily volunteered.

But supposing it is not, what would you do?

You would in due time take your leave, with a dazed feeling somewhat as if you had been forcibly ejected; after a little you would probably come to yourself and say, "What shall I do? I can only go home. I shall go meanwhile to some hotel and enjoy a good dinner, and to-morrow morning I shall take the first train back." But suppose there were no hotel, and no way of getting back? You read my parable? If I had had good news, I should not have held it back so long. This is to break to you that we have had a crushing disappointment in Amboina, and I should be heartily glad to shake its dust from my feet. But that is not easy on an island.

There is no hotel in Amboina, chance travellers being so very rare that there is no inducement to maintain one. Any new arrivals are officials ordered here, who take the place of the one who has left, and step into his house, or receive the hospitality of some other until they can arrange their own home. It was about mid-day when we called on the Resident of Amboina, and during that long walk back from the Residency to the ship it is impossible to describe our feelings. Neither of us dared look the other in the face. But where were we going? To the ship?

It would soon sail. Where was the baggage to be housed, where were we to sleep that night? The subject had to be faced. H. proposed that we should camp in a field, or by the road-side. Fresh from European ways, I stoutly objected. One does not mind setting up a tent on a savage shore, but in a civilised town like Amboina I simply could not bear the idea. I proposed calling at some respectable house, stating our position, and asking to be boarded. H. objected that it was most unlikely that any one would believe us; if the Resident had given us the cold shoulder, they would conclude there was good reason to do the same; he could not face another rebuff.[1]

The steamer, fortunately, did not sail till the morrow, and we remained on it that night. Towards evening, next day, it was suggested to us to apply to the Captain of the Chinese, and to his house we immediately repaired. He welcomed us cordially, and asked us to be seated with him in the verandah. He at once offered the use of a

---

[1] Since I would rather not again refer to this unpleasant subject, I shall here remark that the conduct of the Resident of Amboina was utterly repudiated by the Dutch Government in Java. When we returned, strangers addressed us, and apologised in the name of their countrymen for the blot upon their cherished fame as a hospitable people.

house of his own, just built, and sent one of his
sons along with H., that he might see if it would
suit.   I could only speak very little Malay, not
sufficient to keep up a conversation, but it turned
out that the Chinese gentleman spoke a very little
English.  " Take house one monce, two monce,
tree monce," he said, as he swayed gently to and
fro in his rocking-chair.  You would expect that
from me in my rocking-chair would come the
response, " Thanks ; you are very kind."  It was
excusable : my feelings had been so pent up all
the time, and H. was gone.  I covered my face
with my hands and wept.  A gentle voice close to
me, conveying in its tones a world of sympathy,
said, " You got fazer ? you got mozer ? you got
home ? "  The good old gentleman knew I was
home-sick.  I must ever feel kindly towards his
race for his sake.

Our friend made the house habitable for us,
and I am now writing under its roof.  It would
be a delightful house if furnished ; it looks rather
empty as it is.  But, since we are here only till
we decide on some course of action, it is useless
to think of buying furniture.

The authorities in Batavia expected that the
Government boat would be leaving Amboina for
the Tenimber Islands about the time of our

arrival, and by it we have the privilege to travel.
The Resident returned from that cruise only four
days before we came.   Just lately, a tri-monthly
steamer has commenced to run to New Guinea,
and touches at the Tenimber group.   It is due on
the 18th of June, and we have decided meanwhile to go into the interior of Amboina for
some weeks.   By the aid of our kind friend, the
Chinese gentleman, we procured an old man to
act as cook, and another boy, Jacobus or Kobez :
on their tender mercies we are cast.   My ignor-
ance of Eastern ways and of Malay prevents my
taking any but a very submissive part in our impromptu *menage*.   Two hunters to shoot birds
and collect butterflies are engaged, and we start
early to-morrow.

PASO, 15th May.

This village is only a few hours by prahu from
Amboina.   We started early on a breathless
morning, and thought we should surely see the
marine garden, of which another traveller says,
" No description can do justice to its surpassing
beauty and interest : for once, the reality exceeded the most glowing accounts I had ever
read of the wonders of the coral sea."   But ere
we got out from the shore a breeze sprang up,
causing a ripple which quite hid the bottom,

lessening, however, the heat, as the sun rose in
its strength.

About noon we were thankful to sail close under
the shade of the foliage on the shore. You
must remember that this was my first experience
off the beaten track. Till now I had been in
highly civilised surroundings ; and although in
many cases they have been quite novel, all bore
the trace of European influence. But here was
only the forest, and the quiet shore, and the
native at his daily avocation, quite unconscious
that the small boat passing held beneath its
slight awning eyes more curious than usual.

On arrival at Paso we found the Rajah (the
chief of the village, an official appointed by
Government, without any territorial possession)
preparing to leave for a week, to attend a native
festival. But he has kindly offered us a room
in his house—a bamboo erection, very neat and
clean. The whole village is in a bustle. The
feast is to celebrate the continuance for two
hundred years of amicable relations between
this chief's line and another. The Rajah's
entire household, except the old and infirm,
and about three hundred villagers, set off, after
no little shouting and hurrying to and fro, to
the boats, the final start for which was made

from the church door. The last thing done was
to rake and tidy the space in front of the church,
—"for if proper respect were not paid to Tuan
Allah, perhaps some misfortune might befall
one or other of the prahus."

So we have the village pretty much to ourselves, and there is at most times a stillness like
that of a Scotch Sabbath. Sounds suggest it as
well as silence. The few remaining at home attend church diligently, and singing like that of
a country kirk is frequently heard. It seems
they observe Thursday, Saturday, and Sunday
as holidays : Thursday because Christ died on
that day, Saturday as a day of preparation, and
Sunday as we do. Thursday is observed almost
as rigorously as Sunday. No boisterous play or
shouting is permitted, nor, until after service,
the daily avocations. But this devotion is
purely ceremonial ; their life is not influenced
by the moral precepts of Christianity, and they
have no intelligent comprehension of its tenor.
"Christians" are inveterately lazy, and think
themselves too much the equals of the Europeans
whose religion they have adopted to serve them.
Their change of religion has done much for them
in many ways as a community, but they have
benefited little individually. Intoxication, for-

bidden in the Mohammedan faith, is too frequent, and they are altogether less reliable than their Islamite brethren.

Service is conducted in Malay, and is a copy of the Dutch form of worship, singing, prayer, and sermon following each other. The native clergyman wears a very old and ill-fitting dress-suit, with white tie ; and all the congregation, men and women, wear black, the sign that they are *Sirani* or " Nazarenes."

It is several centuries since the Portuguese brought Christian influences amongst these Malays through the teaching of the Romish Church, and in Paso there is the ruin of a stately edifice in use in the time of Lusitania's power, but now greatly out of keeping with the bamboo erections surrounding it. It is now roofless, except for the arches of a magnificent tree which takes root in the centre of the building, and whose foliage overshadows the massive walls and depends in graceful tracery over the shapely windows.

Paso is situated at the apex of a well-rounded bay, measuring about eight miles, and encircled by richly wooded slopes, behind which mountains tower. There is a sort of method in the laying out of the village, and easy paths cross its length and breadth. One straight before our door leads to the beach, our favourite walk. Through the long hot day, as we sit at work in the verandah, we can see the ever-varying colours on the lovely bay, and far beyond the island of Haruka, the stillness broken only by the monotonous plash of the gentle waves on the shore.

But this is too near a centre of life to be of much use as a hunting-ground, and we are anxious to get on to Waai.

# CHAPTER VII.

WAAI, 30th May.

WE are quite surprised to find ourselves here,
we had such difficulty in getting away. The
Rajah of Paso came back with his company on
the sixth day, all looking inexpressibly jaded
after their prolonged bout of feasting, drinking,
dancing, and broken repose. On such occasions
the true spirit of the native comes out, and in
their revels they are still truly aboriginal. But
on Sunday a large congregation, sobered and
clothed and in their right mind, gathered to
offer thanksgiving for preservation from danger
during the feast.

Their return with noise and shouting seemed
an intrusion on the quiet we had enjoyed, but

we had had great difficulty in getting on in the absence of the Rajah. For three days we had been trying to get away to Waai, but no one would agree to row us. The people are so inveterately lazy that they would much rather do without the wage than earn it. One man might have had his disinclination overcome had we felt inclined to accede to his modest demand of forty rupees, £3, 6s., for rowing us to Tengah-tengah, three hours distant. As half a rupee, or 10d., to each rower, and 5s. for the boat, is the proper fare, you will see that our friend has missed his proper vocation,—he was evidently destined for a London " cabby."

We required an extra box to pack things which we had collected in Paso. After much talking, a man brought an old shabby trunk, so worm-eaten that it would have fallen to pieces with a kick. For this article, worth about sixpence, he asked only six rupees. We did without it.

We were all ready to start on the morning before we really got off. Every box was locked and at the door, when the men who had arranged to take us refused to go unless they had double pay. After spending the whole day in vain attempts to arrange the matter or get another boat, we were told at night that a prahu would return

to Waai next morning at 5 A.M., having come
to Paso with merchandise that evening. At that
hour, accordingly, we were in waiting, only to
discover that it was the very prahu in which we
should have gone the previous morning : the men
had come round, but covered their submission
with this story about its being from Waai. So
much for their veracity.

We had to wait two hours on the beach till
the crew had finally mustered ; but once fairly
away, we soon forgot all the vexations of the few
previous days in the delight of coasting thus
leisurely a tropical shore.

At Tengah-tengah our rowers refused to go
further, saying the strong tide had so fatigued
them that they could not take us all the way.
So we paid them the full fare, at their demand,
in order to save time, and proceeded to ask the
Rajah to order another boat out for us.

The appearance of the Mohammedan village of
Tengah-tengah and the manners of the inhabitants are marvellously different from those of
the Christian villages of Paso and Waai. Though
the people are poor, and much less advanced in
civilised ways, they are courteous and unassum-
ing. Their sole wealth is the bread-fruit tree,
which lines each terrace, the village being built

on a sharp slope. The harvest of the bread-fruit was not yet ready; but as Mr Wallace's account had made us curious to see it, one specimen very nearly ripe was discovered and climbed up for. "It is generally about the size of a melon, a little fibrous towards the centre, but everywhere else quite smooth and puddingy, something in consistence between yeast - dumpling and batter-pudding. We sometimes made curry or stew of it, or fried it in slices; but it is no way so good as simply baked. It may be eaten sweet or savoury; with meat and gravy it is a vegetable superior to any I know, either in temperate or tropical countries. With sugar, milk, butter, or treacle, it is a delicious pudding, having a very slight but characteristic flavour, which, like that of good bread and potatoes, one never gets tired of." Probably ours was badly cooked, or perhaps was not ripe enough. I think it suggests vegetable marrow.

We scarcely understood the Tengah-tengah people : they speak the old language of the country, quite different from the Amboinese Malay, and they wear the *sarong* and headcloth, discarded as derogatory by the Christianised Amboinese. Curious vagaries are played with the hair of the little boys. The head is shaved, except a straight tuft, which is allowed to grow. That of one little fellow seemed specially designed to annoy him; it was just long enough to touch his nose, and appeared constantly to be either tickling that member or getting into his eyes.

Having after some delay obtained a boat and rowers, we started for Waai. When at length, in the middle of the afternoon, we arrived opposite our destination, the whole place seemed as if laid under some enchanter's spell,—not one sign of life was to be seen or heard. We almost felt guilty of desecration as we stole towards the sleep-bound village, and reached the house of the Rajah, who presently appeared in full sleeping costume, evidently bewildered at the unwonted apparition of two white strangers in his verandah. I longed to say, "How are you, Mr Rip Van Winkle?" Having explained the object of our visit, we came to terms with him for an unoccupied house, a stone erection, a short distance from his own dwelling. We have plenty of room, but a bamboo-pile hut is much preferable to an occasionally opened stone building. The soft sand floor is damp, and lacks an air of cleanliness.

The village of Waai is laid out in squares,

divided by perfectly straight streets. The gardens open into these streets, which are lined with overarching trees, and margined by ditches edged with pink crocus-like plants. The credit of this is in a measure due to the efforts of the people, but luxuriant nature does much. With hand-to-hand work and sympathetic treatment, Waai might be a garden of romance. I like to be astir early, to meet the inhabitants wending under the grand avenues towards the stream : with the intermingling colours of the garments of the loitering water-carriers and the soft lights, the scene is somewhat Italian-like.

The stream comes fresh from the mountains, cool and sparkling, and is met in the village by a shallow pond, above which water for domestic use is taken, and in which the villagers bathe and wash. In the centre of the pond is an enclosure with house attached. This is the Rajah's bathing-place, and its use is permitted to us—a delightful luxury.

In the pond the children disport themselves like fishes; mites who can just run can swim and enjoy the fun like the others. The elders make the bath more of a business, and I must say I have considerable respect for their cleanliness. They use a stone in lieu of soap, carefully

choosing a particular kind from the smooth
pebbles on the edge; and when they have indus-
triously bathed, they dip the finger in the silvery
sand, and with it polish the teeth!

There is a large church in Waai, quite out of
proportion in size and grandeur to the population and intellectual elevation of the place. We
came on it by chance one Sunday morning, and
were so amused and interested that we did not
notice the congregation gathering. Then we
hurried away, for beside the decent company we
felt ashamed of our travel-stained and un-Sunday-
like garments. The area of the church is set
with cane-bottomed chairs instead of fixed pews.
On one side, raised a few feet above the floor, is
a suite of seats reserved for the Rajah's use,
canopied, carved, and richly gilded, with his coat
of arms emblazoned in front. The pulpit is also
much carved and gilded, and the church altogether is tastefully fitted, and is abundantly
lighted with petroleum lamps. The services are
conducted in High Malay by a European mis-
sionary (he is absent at present on a tour to
distant stations), and in his absence by the
native schoolmaster, who with moderate regu-
larity instructs the children five days a-week.
Amboinese Rajahs keep no state, and wear no

special dress, except on Sundays. To-day we
had the honour of seeing the potentate of Waai
proceed to church in state. He was attired in
black trousers—which, being rather short, displayed a length of white cotton stocking—black
"swallow-tail" coat, made for a stouter and
taller individual than himself, probably his
father, and a beaver hat, tall and narrow, of an
ancient pattern, while over his head a youth
carried his gilded state umbrella. The whole
population attended the service, all of them in
black calico attire.

This black dress is a relic of Portuguese influence. The Rajah of Paso informs us that the
garments pass from one generation to another,
being worn only on Sundays and holidays.
The freshness is renewed at will by dipping in a
dye of their own making, after which the
garment is hung in the breeze and repeatedly
brushed one way to bring on the pretty gloss.

Some women wear a beaded belt, and we learn
that these are wives of burghers—*i.e.*, men who
do no forced labour. A soldier who has served
a long term is made a burgher, and his wife
wears a beaded belt. Wives of non-burghers
wear combs, which mark their position. The
women's dress, you must remember, is in the

form of *sarong* and *kabia*. The men have ill-shapen trousers coming to the ankle, and the loose *kabia* jacket, all of the same black material. Those in mourning are distinguished by a long *kabia*, which must be very uncomfortable in walking, since it trips up the wearer at every step. For nearest relations mourning is worn a year, and six months for those more distantly connected. The women of the Rajah's household are an exception to the wearing of black on special occasions ; and they must wear diamond ear-rings, a gold comb, and shoes.

I am distressed by the appearance of the children in all these parts. A healthy-looking child is a rare sight, nearly all being afflicted with an unnatural distension of the stomach, caused by the almost unvaried diet of sago, eaten without any further cooking than the baking which moulds it into cakes. The arms and legs are miserably thin, every rib shows clearly, and there is often a sad expression along with this unhealthy state. And yet the men are strong and sinewy enough.

Sago as they use it would be unrecognisable to you. The first time I saw it was as we rowed up the bay of Amboina : the men were eating hard rust-coloured cakes, which seemed to me

made of sawdust.   And such they in a sense
are.   Unlike rice or barley, sago is not the fruit
of a tiny stem,—it is the pith of the trunk of a
great tree.   The tree is felled, the pith—a soft
fibrous wood—is scraped out, then it is beaten
fine, and laid in a trough with water to steep.
The water passes through a sieve into another
trough, carrying with it the starch in the wood,
and this settles at the bottom.   The sediment is
sago in its first stage—a fine powder, which is at
once packed into cylinder-like cases for export.
The neighbouring island of Ceram supplies most
of the   surrounding   islands   with   their   daily
bread, and while we were at Paso boats frequently landed laden with this product.

In these cylinders the sago forms into a caked
mass.   To bake it, it is broken up and dried,
when it becomes a fine flour ; this is placed in a
heated mould with some five or six divisions,
and from these the baked cakes are turned out.
When hot they are soft and very sweet ; when
cold they become hard, and are in this condition the daily food of the natives.

Dried in the sun the cakes will keep for years.
We mean to take a store of them to Timor-laut ;
indeed our men could ill subsist without them—
they are accustomed to them all their lives, and

prefer them to rice. Soaked and boiled, the cakes make a delicious pudding : we have it daily, sweetened with the coarse native sugar and eaten with cocoa-nut milk. These combined have a flavour I would not give for the most delicate pudding you could offer me. Sago loses greatly in taking the form of the article of commerce, just as exceedingly refined sugar or flour loses the special flavour of its rougher state.

Although little used by the natives, tapioca is also abundant here. We cannot perceive any resemblance even in flavour to the delicate article familiar at home tables. Tapioca, again, is a root of oblong shape, and about twice the size of a very large potato. We use it as a vegetable, cut in pieces and boiled, and thus treated it is not bad.

The variety of fish is surprising. All sizes and shapes abound ; the Rajah declares that he does not exaggerate in stating that 800 different kinds come into their nets. A celebrated Dutch specialist has given a catalogue of 780 species found in Amboina, a number almost equal to those of all the seas and rivers of Europe. Our choice ranges from the size of minnows to that of huge cod, and the quality is excellent.

Fowls are abundant also ; but as they live

simply on what they can pick up, they are
generally rather meagre.  Broods in every stage
of development range in the gardens and by the
roadsides.  I believe the owner never gives them
a thought till they are of marketable size.  There
are no cows here, but the natives need not lack
flesh ; there are the wild pig, the deer, and the
cuscus.  This last is a curious creature the size
of a hare, but as different as may be in habit
and action from that agile quadruped.  The
cuscus seems to be ever sleeping, and lives clinging to the stems and branches of trees, feeding
solely on the leaves.  We have two young ones,
which I carefully feed and tend, and which
interest me greatly.  They grasp their food
between the two fore paws, and eat—I was going
to say like squirrels, but there is nothing frisky
or vivacious in their movements ; they munch
with great gravity, staring pathetically the while
from their bright eyes.  My pets do not seem to
thrive ; they suffer from being out of their
element probably.  The young are brought up
as kangaroos are, in the mother's pouch.

Fruits and vegetables abound ; with a judicious
use of the various kinds of food at command, the
natives need not suffer from the painful-looking
sores and eruptions which disfigure such a large

proportion of them. To tend a wound does not
seem to occur to them : they walk with it bare,
and exposed to accidental knocks and scratches
in the forest, as well as to the irritation of flies
and ants, and the same sore often remains un-
healed for years.

One cannot restrain a little mild indignation
against the Waai people. Their naturally beautiful village could be so beautified ; abundance,
even wealth, is pressed upon them by the luxuriant productiveness of nature ; and yet all
they care for is to be allowed to vegetate. No
energy, no aspiration, ever disturbs them. As I
have said, civilising influences have not really
raised their moral status ; they have become
more independent—not, however, for their own
good. I fancy it is beneficial for such a people
to be under an autocratic ruler. The Rajah tells
us his authority is now a mere name. He was
once called to attend a conference at Amboina.
The men who rowed him "struck" half-way,
and turned the boat homewards. They were
arrested, and sentenced to eight days' imprison-
ment, after which they came back with such a
tale of the good time they had had—feeding
well without any labour or cost, and playing
cards all day with pleasant companions—that

more harm than good was effected by the punishment.

That they are not sensitive in conscience, we find to our cost. Their end in life at present is to obtain all they can out of us; and in pursuance of this aim they beset our door with all sorts of things for sale—insects, birds, plants, food, &c.—which they offer at prices that are a constant source of amusement to us. A meagre chicken is offered for 1s. 8d., while the highest price that would be given in the Amboina market would be one-third of this. For a fair-sized fish a rupee and a-half is complacently asked, though the vendor takes 60 cents, and knows he has had a fair bargain. We met a woman by the shore bringing a basketful of tapioca roots from the gardens, and we tried to bargain for some, but thought her price of 25 cents each rather exorbitant. Next day we were offered at our own door four for 10 cents.

And the guile of those children! They walk boldly up to us in the verandah with a bright flower, which has dropped from some tree, stuck upon a twig pulled from a hedge—"Fifty cents, master. Very rare; never seen before!"

Another follows with a butterfly whose wings

are all bruised and broken, and a beetle muti-
lated beyond having any further value.

H. "I do not care for any which are not
perfect."

"But, master, this is the kind of the insects
in Waai. There are many such here, I assure
you."

H. often gives a trifle for worthless specimens,
that they may not be discouraged from seeking,
and perchance finding something rare. When a
little fellow has made up his mind to a certain
sum and receives less, you should see the disdain
with which he flings down the coin; and, if it
were worth picking up, we might find the flower
or insect on the path, thrown down by him as he
walks off laughing contemptuously.

I am beginning to enter into the joys of a
naturalist, and have grown quite learned in long
names of birds and insects, and can help H. in
labelling and arranging. The later hours of every
afternoon are looked forward to by both of us as
the most pleasant of the day, when the hunters'
spoils are displayed for our admiration. The
gay parrots and beautiful kingfishers, the curious
maleos, whose terra-cotta eggs are a table luxury,
and those wonderfully plumaged pigeons, give
us special delight. Strolling along the bay, on

whose beach the east wind has been throwing a wealth of sponges, hydroids, and shells, we spend many hours examining them and watching the fields of shore-crabs, with their richly coloured pincer limbs, and the curious fishes which come up out of the water and hop along the shore in their odd way.

When H. goes with the men to the forest, I accompany as far as I am able. Several shallow rivulets find their outlet round Waai, and there is no way of reaching the surrounding country except by crossing some one of them. When we start, I am carried through the streams by Lopez if there are no stepping-stones. But these boulders, thrown in by the natives, and easily grasped by their unbooted feet, are simply a snare to us; we invariably slip off them into the water. The rest of the walk is then taken without any regard to boots and stockings, and on my return alone I splash quite unconcernedly through the streams.

Sometimes the forest path leads through a deep glade under high-arching trees, where the undergrowths are lit up by rich blossom or gorgeous tree-fruit; sometimes through stretches of open field, from which we can look out on the pleasing scenery of the environs. I find H.'s warning, not to expect a wonderful profusion of fine flowers in the tropics, not to have been needless. Speaking of Sumatra, he says : " This [the flower] is just one of the products of the Garden of the Sun that the traveller fails to see, unless he search very well and very closely. The vegetation at the lower elevations leaves the impression of a tangled heterogeneous mass of foliage of every shape and shade, mingled together in such unutterable confusion that not one single plant stands out in anything like its own individuality in his mind. The great forest-trees are too high for him to be able to see whether they bear either fruit or flowers. It is only on rare occasions—and then the sight repays him for many a weary mile—that he alights on a grand specimen whose top is ablaze with crimson or gold; more generally he knows that some high tree is performing its functions by seeing broken petals or fallen fruit spread over yards of the ground. Hours and hours, sometimes days even, I have traversed a forest-bounded road without seeing a blossom gay enough to attract admiration. A vast amount of tropical vegetation has small, inconspicuous flowers, of a more or less green colour, so that when they do occur the eye fails to detect them readily.

The fresh green, the rich pink, and even scarlet, of the opening leaves are beautiful beyond description, and the autumn-tinted foliage never ceases through all the seasons; but I had little idea as I rounded the cape of Gibraltar, leaving to the north of me purple hills of heather, scarlet fields of poppies, and rich parterres starred with cistus and orchids, with anemones and geraniums, and sweet with aromatic shrubs and herbs, that I should encounter nothing half so rich or bright amid all the profusion of the summer of the world."

Even the flowers cultivated in gardens do not yield the pleasure of a bouquet at home. They are either scentless, or scent so heavily that they are sickening. They fade quickly when gathered; but they are really scarcely suitable for an ornament in a room,—they need their own setting of ample greenery to tone their gorgeousness.

# CHAPTER VIII.

WAAI — THE RAINS — THE RAJAH — NATIVE SKIFFS — FISH
" MAZES "—AQUEOUS LIFE—DANGEROUS CURRENTS.

*1st June.*

RAIN has commenced in earnest, and we take
rather ill with the restraint of staying indoors.
The roof leaks badly, and there is scarcely a dry
yard under the verandah. Two of the men have
had fever, and have added to the dismal aspect
of things by constant moaning and groaning.
Pedros is kept in good humour with an occasional
glass of gin. He does his clumsy best to fill the
place of our cook, and waits on the sick, but we
shall be glad to return to our normal ways.
Pedros is a very good fellow, besides being an
excellent bird-skinner. We are anxious that he
should go with us to Timor-laut, but he cannot
make up his mind to part from his family. He
is rather fond of gin, but never gets intoxicated.
To-day he was picking some seeds, the contact

with which caused an irritating tickling on the
hands. To allay this we poured some gin over
them. What dismay overspread his countenance
to see the precious potion thus wasted! When
he was called and saw the bottle, he evidently
thought he was to be offered a drink as compen-
sation for the discomfort he was suffering. All
he could do was to lick his hands!

Sometimes it clears about sundown, when we
hasten out, generally to the shore, where we
need not brush through dripping foliage. One
evening a scene of rare beauty gave us an hour
of deep delight. Waai is situated on a wide bay,
facing the island of Haruka. The lofty peaks of
Ceram shut in the view to the left, to the right
is the narrow outlet to the sea beyond, and
numerous foliage-clad islands stud the enclosed
expanse, which, but for the outlet between Haruka
and the mainland, might be a small inland sea.
We stood on the shore at ebb-tide, in front of a
background of lofty trees of richest green which
belted the shore for miles, the dusky figures of
the natives in their gay clothing relieving the
scene as they wend their way homeward bearing
their burdens, or stand fishing on the water's
edge. The peaks of Ceram rise grand and grey,
Haruka shows intense dark-blue, the opening is

just catching the crimson of the sunset, the
motionless glittering sea is reflecting the golden
sheen; piled masses of purple, and crimson, and
pink, and soft grey, and pure white cloud are
banked up even to the enclosing vault of the
blue heaven, where a few stars peep through,
"candles to the pale moon" that shows occasionally between the shifting clouds. It seemed but
a minute ere the descent of a mountain blast
changed the scene to a grey, stormy aspect,—the
sea rises in ripples, the tall cocoa-palms fring-
ing the shore sway in the breeze, and the whole
forest moans in the disturbance. While we yet
stand admiring, this phase of beauty gives way
to the placid moonlight. During the short
struggle day has died; night takes its place,
dominated by the full moon, whose light shim-
mers on the now smooth sea and sheds its
rays over the whole prospect. Which is the
lovelier,—the rich glory of the Eastern sunset
or the soft intensity of its moonlight? We
turn away, compensated for many discomforts
of travel and pangs of home-sickness.

The Rajah is a quiet unobtrusive man, and
during our stay we have seen little of him. Yesterday, however, we had more of his company
than we cared for. There has been for some

time a dearth of alcohol in Waai, and on the arrival of fresh supplies he has evidently been making up for previous privation. He came about eight in the morning, inspired with a valiant desire to go to the chase, and begged the loan of a gun and some powder and shot. But he had indulged so deeply that the intoxicant had made him purposeless, and it was hours before he rose to go. H. sent one of our men in his rear to see that he did not by mistake shoot himself, or some of his equally incapable companions, and we were relieved when towards evening they all came back safe. The chief stumbled to a chair, from which he did not manage to rise for hours, prating on with thick utterance till we were heartily tired. How changed from his sober hours !

Natives sail round the coast, and even to the adjacent islands, in tiny skiffs, scooped from a log, which they have under such control that they are in perfect safety. Some are fitted with outriggers, which make capsizing impossible, but they prefer them without this incumbrance, for on coming in, riding on the crest of a wave, the rower picks up his boat and marches off with it on his shoulders. The usual size is just wide enough to seat one, and about five feet in length.

One evening when the sea was perfectly calm, we hailed a man who was approaching the shore to take us out to some fishing "mazes." These mazes consist of lines of close bamboo palisades, which terminate in deep water in a circular well, where fish that have entered during high tide are enclosed and captured, escape being prevented by the ebb. On these palisades a species of water-bird, of which H. was anxious to get a specimen, settles every evening. There is always, even in calmest seas, a slight surf on the shore, and there is no time to lose if you will catch a boat when it comes in on a wave before it recedes again. There was just room for us both; the rower had to perch himself at the stern, where he propelled the boat with a single oar. It was not a very comfortable sail, but we were thoroughly compensated. The narrow skiff cuts the water without dimming the surface by ripples, the oar disturbs only the water behind, and in a calm sea the wonders of the sea-gardens can be seen to perfection. I was fairly excited with delight. I too could say that " the reality exceeded the most glowing accounts I had ever read of the wonders of a coral sea." Such wondrous forms of aqueous life, sprays and spikes, clusters and wreaths of

G

coral, I had never formed any conception of. Brilliant blue and red sponges and æsthetic-coloured jelly-fish took the place of flowers in the nooks of the chasms and sides of the hillocks of the uneven surface of the marine gardens; while fishes, banded, spotted, and streaked with brightest hues, darted out and in from their hiding-places. We found that our boatman was a diver, and he went below for anything which caught our fancy, amusing us greatly as he swam about seeking at our direction the coral or fish we wanted, and came puffing with it to the surface. Although the native makes no scruple of jumping into the sea to pick up his boat, and wades through a swollen river without a thought, all seem to shrink from rain. In the rainy season the clothesless children go to fetch water under a large leaf, which opens exactly as does a sheet of note-paper, and under this same sort of covering the grown people carry their wares. Some have a hat of such dimensions, that it also serves the purpose of an umbrella; without some such protection no one stirs from the door.

To-morrow we return to Amboina, if fine. The roads will soon be very difficult, and our house lets in rain, so that it is most uncomfortable. We must go by land to Paso, a march of fourteen miles. It would be much easier to go by sea, were the currents not dangerous owing to the state of the monsoon. We thought this was a shifting excuse, until we made an attempt to go to the island of Haruka, on the opposite side of the bay, when we had a narrow escape from being swamped. A strong breeze suddenly sprang up, and when we got out into the open sea, our boat seemed a very plaything on the high waves which were running, and the men declared that it would become unmanageable if we persisted in crossing. After the boat had twice been all but capsized, we had to abandon our project and return.

# CHAPTER IX.

DEPARTURE FROM WAAI—THROUGH THE FOREST—BRILLIANT
COLOURS — BACK TO PASO — VOYAGE TO AMBOINA —
GAIETIES — THE TOWN OF AMBOINA — TRACES OF THE
PORTUGUESE—EVENING SCENES—OUR CHINESE FRIEND—
MANGOSTEENS—THE DURIAN—WAITING FOR THE STEAMER
—*TRASSI*—*EN ROUTE* FOR TIMOR-LAUT—A RAJAH PILOT.

AMBOINA, 12*th June.*

WE really got away from Waai on the 9th.
The previous evening the Rajah had been ear-
nestly enjoined to have everything in readiness,
and with the first streaks of dawn we were
waiting to start. However, only thirteen of the
eighteen men necessary to carry me and the
baggage turned up, and before the five defaulters
were routed out and the loads arranged in lots
on the carrying-poles, the cool hours of the
morning were gone, and the march was commenced when it was already too hot for comfort.
My palanquin was an old-fashioned, cumbrous

affair, formerly used by the Rajah and his
family. One-third of the size would have held
me, and would have been less troublesome in the
forest, where it was too wide for the paths, and
caused the men great discomfort from stumbling
against roots and twigs. When heavily laden,
carriers proceed at a sharp trot, urging each
other on with shouts and indulging in constant
groans. Now and again, when there was shade,
I came out and walked; but though this was a
pleasure to me, and a rest to H., who had not
been on the march for many months, and found
this rather trying, for he would keep a steadying
hand on the palanquin, it was a great hindrance
to our progress.

On we pressed, sometimes through a sparse
wood of the white-barked cajeput-tree, by a
pleasant grass-grown road, sometimes through
stretches of alang-alang grass, terribly trying
to the men, for the feet must be lifted as if
wading through waves, and it reflects cruelly
the fierce heat of the sun, while the sharp blades
cut their legs. Sometimes we could see the
distant hills and the surrounding fine scenery;
again our path lay through the arbour-like shade
of the overarching forest, and we were shut in
to the beauty of giant stems and profuse en-

tangled foliage. Twice we had to cross rivers, and frequently descended into rocky gorges where the rivulets were swollen into torrents, and down the clayey descent to which it was almost impossible for the men to keep a footing. One would go suddenly on his back, causing a lurch to the palanquin, which would almost send me flying out. I should greatly have preferred walking, but it was evident that it would be impossible for me to keep my feet in the slimy mud. So I lay flat down and tried to think I was having a luxurious time, while I watched the beautiful ferns and mosses in the rocky ledges, and enjoyed to the full the comparative cool of the damp atmosphere in the deep shade, before we should again emerge into the strong heat of the blazing sun.

I do not wish to be ever raving about the wondrous beauty of tropical scenery. I would not rouse in you any discontent with our "ain countrie." The tempered softness of these sweet June evenings you are now enjoying, that harmonious blending of richest colours which I can recall in a moorland scene in autumn, are as perfectly satisfying as any picture I could portray. But when we emerged from the deep forest shade, the prospect before us of the brightness of the bay at noonday struck me as freshly as if I had for the first time looked upon that peculiar brilliancy of colouring which only a vertical sun can lend. Was ever sea so blue?—did ever waves display a purer emerald in their graceful curl, or crown themselves with crests so white?—was ever outline of hills so clear, or foliage so graceful as that of the shadowy palms we halted under?

While the carriers rested, our men fetched some cocoa-nuts, and we all together enjoyed the cooling draught and lunched off the blanc-mange-like pulp. When we reached the Rajah's house at Paso it was exactly noon. Thus we had been four hours in covering fourteen miles,—not a bad record, since the men were heavily laden, and crossing rivers and descending into torrent-beds required cautious walking. Lopez had been sent on to get a boat in readiness, for we had heard that the tide was high in Amboina harbour at 3 P.M., and congratulated ourselves that we should get on after an hour or two of rest in a shady room. Vain expectation! The Rajah was from home, and no one knew of a boat large enough for us and our baggage. After hours of fruitless effort, the Rajah returned, and at once peremptorily ordered out a boat,

shouting as if thus alone he could enforce his
command,—he assured us apologetically that it
was indeed so.   The sun went down, rain commenced to fall heavily, and after securing ourselves and the baggage as well as possible from
the drenching torrent, we got away at 8 P.M.
It has taken days to dry the contents of the
cases, many of the birds being hopelessly spoiled.
We were as wet as if we had come to Amboina
swimming at the stern of the boat.   It was a
very unsafe " dug-out," with no outriggers ; and
though worn out from the long fatiguing day,
we dared not beguile a part of the way in sleep,
for fear of capsizing it by an unguarded movement.   Luckily the sea was as smooth as glass,
and we kept ourselves awake watching the
trickling rain dropping in phosphorescent sparks
on the water, and the luminous zigzag path of
the frightened fishes darting from below our
keel, while in concert with this brilliant aqueous
illumination the torches of the fishermen blazed
on the banks.   Arriving about midnight, we
were perplexed to find the door of our old
quarters unopened.   One of the men had gone
on by road to cook supper and make all needful
preparations ; but instead of food and light,
only silence and darkness awaited us.   The man

had gone among his friends, and forgotten all about us. At last the key was obtained by rousing our kind old Chinaman, and we at length got under cover. The little furniture that was in the house had been removed during our absence of a month; but we found a boat-sail in a corner of one of the rooms, which, spread on the stone floor, had to serve that night for a resting-place.

We found Amboina in the bustle of preparing for a demonstration in honour of the visit of a member of the Council of Netherlands India. Floral arches, gracefully draped with palm-leaves and tastefully festooned with flowers, decorate the streets, which are illuminated at night. Even the poorest house in the native quarter has a dammar light flaring on a pedestal of the stem of the sago-palm stripped of its sheath.

All the surrounding rajahs are required to be present in the town, with a certain number of followers. At Waai there was daily practice of a dance to be performed on the great occasion, at which I was a frequent onlooker. It was an old war-dance, with some slight semblance of savage wildness and vehemence. The elder performers seemed to feel rather ashamed of their grotesque dress, but the lads were by no means

averse to the gay colours and profuse ornaments
they wore. Gold lace, quantities of gilt paper,
and red and blue streamers, with their bright
*sarongs* and plumed hats, gave them a really picturesque appearance ; and when they capered in
the dance, brandishing their harmless spears and
beating on their needless shields, with leaps and
yells simulating the wildest excitement, the imagination was not greatly strained to picture the
old reality. Surely every fowl in the neighbourhood must have been sacrificed to provide feather
decorations for their hats, shields, and spears.
Each performer had attached to his person some
half-dozen lace-trimmed pocket-handkerchiefs,
incongruous belongings of the occupants of bamboo huts, which were not used to wipe the
streaming perspiration, but were merely part of
their trappings.

We had no part in the gaieties consequent on
this visit ; but it yielded us an enjoyment of its
kind, which quite outweighed any feelings of
bitterness at our exclusion. Social pariahs, we
looked on from the skirt of the crowd, and in
watching their amusements, their manner of
enjoying them, and their expression while thus
engaged, we got an insight into the native character not to be had from any other standpoint.

Amboina is one of the most salubrious of
towns. It is situated on a long, river-like arm
of the sea, and commands a fine prospect over
the water to the mountains beyond, while it is
encircled by verdure-clad slopes, to which shady,
arbour-like roads lead from the centre of the
town. Along the shore are stores, factories, and
the dwellings of the trading portion of the community. Between this quarter and the pleasant
environ where the European dwellings stand, is
a stretch of greensward, the parade-ground of
the troops and the promenade of Europeans, for
whose pleasure the military band discourses
music twice a-week. To the left of the sward is
the fort, enclosed within which are the post-
office and Government offices. To the right is a
club, where the 'Illustrated London News,' the
'Graphic,' and other high-class periodicals lie for
perusal. The most elegant mansions in the
town belong not to Europeans, but to Chinese
and Arabs, who have every scope for exercising
their powers as money amassers, for Amboina
has been more or less a centre of European occupation for some 350 years. When the Dutch
took the rule in these parts from the Portuguese,
they made Amboina the clove-garden of the
Moluccas; but although there has now been

communication with the Dutch for 250 years, the Portuguese element predominates in the old Christian population. This nation had a wonderful power of impressing its national characteristics on the peoples it subjected. Traces of its influence are yet indicated in habits and words — *nyora* (signora), *lenço* (handkerchief), *cadeira* (chair), and many domestic terms, being plainly Portuguese. Although the Amboinese now profess the Protestant faith, at feasts and on gay occasions they preserve the processions and music of the Catholic Church, curiously mingled with the gongs and dances of the aborigines.

The weather is simply delightful. Every day it gets more and more into the rainy season, but not sufficiently yet to cause discomfort. Even at mid-day a fresh breeze blows, and at evening one might call the climate temperate. After the hottest hour we are ready to set out, and have already become familiar with the town and its outskirts. We frequently meet the stream of Mohammedans gathering for evening worship at the mosque. The wealthy Arab comes along with measured tread, his ablutions already performed, and fresh in his flowing white robes : his poorer brethren come rushing up, press in

among their fellows at the bath, and hurry with
a hop, skip, and jump to join their fellow-wor-
shippers in the holy place, adjusting by the way
the clean *sarong* or pushing the arms into the
jacket. How we have enjoyed gazing into the
lamplit churches, into shops and dwellings, and,
most of all, loitering in the market-place. This
spot is exceedingly picturesque. The booths
form a square, in whose centre a great tree
spreads its giant arms. A lamp flares at every
stall; and standing back in the shade—the only
Europeans in the jostling crowd—we have found
it an unfailing source of interest to listen to the
bargaining that goes on, and to read the native
mind from the expression on the faces of buyer
and seller. In the dark street, lit by the bright
stoves of street-vendors roasting Indian corn and
other favourite food of the natives, we hear from
an open window the monotonous drawl of many
voices repeating simultaneously the Koran; while
from another proceeds the excited merriment of
gamblers. The Chinese have an elegant joss-
house, which has recently been constantly illuminated to celebrate the birthday of one of their
gods. He is a funny-looking little image, who
dwells among a number of lady and baby gods
in the middle case of three which fill one end of

the building.   We were told with pride that he
is "hundreds of years old."   Before the case in
which he is kept are piles of food, an offering
to him.   The worshippers feast in an apartment
behind, where groaning tables are spread for
them.   They sit smoking and talking in the
sacred edifice as if they were out visiting.

Occasionally we pay a visit to our old friend
the Chinese gentleman, and enjoy pleasant and
instructive chats on all subjects.   He showed us
a bundle of tortoise-shell—thirteen pieces in all,
unpolished and produced from a homely calico
bag—which he says is worth a thousand rupees.
Such a possession, it seems, is an indication of
prosperity and a guarantee of luck.   This good
gentleman is the owner of much property in
Amboina : he is the chief baker, and keeps a
number of cows for the supply of milk to
Europeans.

It is now the season of the mangosteen.   I
had heard much of this fruit before coming to
the East, and my expectation was on very
tiptoe from reading one traveller's opinion that
"this beautiful fruit is the epitome of all gastronomic delights, meeting in subtlest harmony
upon the palate, a fragrant fleeting poem ; " and
that, " if there were more of this fruit on the

earth, there would be need for neither churches nor jails, for there would be no sin." Now this is scarcely fair to stay-at-home people. You have really its equivalent in a luscious peach, in a fine ripe jargonelle pear, or in a strawberry at its best; and if you can imagine a combination of these three, you have an idea of how the mangosteen itself tastes. It is considered to be the most delicious of tropical fruits, and simply as a product of nature it is very beautiful to look upon. It is as large as a medium-sized or rather small apple, of the same shape, and of a dusky plum colour. The rind is nearly half an inch in thickness; gently press it and it opens, disclosing the pure white fruit lying in a fleshy fibrous-streaked bed of rose-pink. The pulp, a juicy mouthful, is sweet, and melts away in the mouth, leaving a single stone.

We have also just now the durian, of which Mr Wallace says that it is worth a voyage to the East to taste it, giving it the place of honour as the king of fruits, with the orange for queen. Although I have an unmixed respect for all this traveller says—he portrays with such absolute fidelity—I cannot indorse this statement. But we are not in a position to judge from his standpoint: we did not meet with it fresh

fallen in the forest, where its strong odour could
not overpower, and in circumstances in which
most gastronomic comforts are necessarily denied.
Perhaps in his place I also should be inclined to
say that " it is unsurpassed as a food of the most
exquisite flavour."

This fruit is not allowed a place at table in
hotels or civilised households.   It has an odour
which I can only describe as the quintessence
of onions, but this is concentrated in the rind.
If broken open at some distance from the house,
the contents may be eaten without nausea ; and
with some claret or a little brandy over it, the
custard-like pulp is certainly delicious.   I have
never seen the tree, but learn that the durian
" grows on a large lofty forest-tree, somewhat
resembling an elm."   The fruit may be compared to a cocoa-nut with the outer husk : it is
almost of the same shape, perhaps less oval, and
it is very spiny.

The durian is like no other fruit from which I
could offer a comparison : it contains no juice, it
is not sweet, it is not acid ; it is a food more
than a refreshment.   One contains enough to
afford a very satisfactory lunch, and in the process of discussing the custard-coloured pulp,
which has the consistency of an ice-cream, you

find some seeds as large as chestnuts. We went into the courtyard, where we had instructed Kobez to break one open, to examine the rind, and despite the odour I could not refrain from drawing my finger over the lovely lining of the cells in which the pulp had been embedded, to discover if it felt as satiny as it looked.

*28th June.*

We are still in Amboina, in hourly expectation of the steamer. It is already ten days overdue, and we must perforce endure the discomfort of living with our boxes packed, sure that it must come to-morrow. We shall doubtless be able to laugh over this period when we recall it in after years, but at present it is very trying to be thus losing time. Nearly two months ago we were thus far towards the goal of our journey; our men are idle, and our funds are melting away. We dare not go a day's journey, or even a few hours from the house, lest the vessel should come in the meantime; we have no definite occupation, and cannot help fretting. One great pleasure we have. The steamer of the 13th brought to Amboina an old friend of H.'s in Sumatra, Dr Julius Machik, who, posted to the charge of the military hospital, has come

H

with his family to reside here. We were one
day sitting in our comfortless dwelling, engrossed in writing, when a hearty voice hailed
us from the window; and now our pleasant
intercourse with the Machiks brings an element
of regret into our heartfelt longing to be off.
They are in a temporary dwelling until the
large house they have chosen on the plain is
ready for occupation. But this has not hin-
dered their hospitality, and daily comes a
humorous invitation, generally in the form of
a prescription, to join them at some meal.

We have engaged Kobez to continue with us
as cook, and Lopez and Carl go as hunters and
bird-skinners. These last are excellent men.
Kobez is not a great acquisition; but, as you
may suppose, a good domestic readily finds a
good situation, and would not undertake the
makeshifts of life on a savage island. Kobez
is very anxious to take a store of *trassi*.

"What is *trassi?*" Hear how H. details his
first acquaintance with it, while in Java, shortly
after his arrival in the East. "A vile odour
which permeates the air within a wide area of
the market-place proceeds from a compound
sold in round black balls, called *trassi*. My
acquaintance with it was among my earliest ex-

periences of housekeeping at Genteng. Having
got up rather late one Sunday morning—an
opportunity taken by one of my boys to go
unknown to me to the market, which I had
not then visited — I was discomfited by the
terrific and unwonted odour of decomposition.
'My birds have begun to stink!' I exclaimed
to myself. Hastily fetching down the box in
which they were stored, I minutely examined
and sniffed over every skin, giving myself in
the process inflammation of the nostrils and
eyes for a week after, from the amount of
arsenical soap I inhaled; but all of them
seemed in perfect condition. In the neighbouring jungle, though I diligently searched
half the morning, I could find no dead carcase,
and nothing in the 'kitchen-midden,' where
somehow I seemed nearer the source; but at
last in the kitchen itself I ran it to ground
in a compact parcel done up in a banana
leaf.

" 'What on the face of creation is this?' I said
to the cook, touching it gingerly.

" 'Oh! master, that is *trassi.*'

" '*Trassi?*  Whatever is *trassi?*'

" 'Good for eating, master—in stew.'

" 'Have *I* been eating it?'

" ' Certainly, master ; it is *most* excellent (*enak sekali*).'

" ' You fool ! Do you wish to poison me and to die yourself ? '

" ' May I have a goitre (*daik gondok*), master, but it *is* excellent ! ' he asseverated, taking hold of the foreskin of his throat, by the same token that a countryman at home would swear, ' *As sure's death !* '

" Notwithstanding these vehement assurances, I made it disappear in the depths of the jungle, to the horror of the boy, who looked wistfully after it, and would have fetched it back, had I not threatened him with the direst penalties if I discovered any such putridity in my house again. I had then to learn that in every dish, native or European, that I had eaten since my arrival in the East, this Extract of Decomposition was mixed as a spice, and it would have been difficult to convince myself that I would come by - and - by knowingly to eat it daily without the slightest abhorrence. Dampier, who mentions it in his ' Voyage,' seems to have formed his acquaintance with it in a more philosophic spirit, for he describes it in these terms : —' As a composition of a strong savour, yet a very delightsome dish to the natives. To make

it they throw a mixture of shrimps and small
fish into a sort of weak pickle made with salt
and water, and put into a tight earthen vessel.
The pickle being thus weak, it keeps not the
fish firm and hard, neither is it probably so
designed, for the fish are never gutted. Therefore in a short time they turn all to a mash in
the vessel; and when they have lain thus a
good while, so that the fish is reduced to pulp,
they then draw off the liquor into fresh jars
and preserve it for use. The masht fish that
remains behind is called *trassi*. 'Tis rank
scented; yet the taste is not altogether unpleasant, but rather savoury after one is a little
used to it.'"

*7th July*, en route *for* TIMOR-LAUT.

We are at last on our way, with all our
belongings and our three men. We were
nearly off with only two, Kobez almost manag-
ing to give us the slip. He came on board with
us, and was most attentive until everything
was in order; then he must have run away and
hid amongst his friends. The two others went
to seek him, and put some half-dozen native
policemen on his track. Hearing of the pursuit,
he came on board about 3 A.M., looking very
innocent, and saying he was waiting on shore

till the moon rose to let him see to join the ship. There was bright moonlight at 10 the previous evening.

There is one European passenger on board besides ourselves, a Dutch gentleman, inspector of native schools, who, from the wide knowledge thus gained of the people and their customs, is a most interesting companion. The pilot is a remarkable character. There is no chart of these seas for the ship's course, and since this old man has sailed them from his boyhood, and is perfectly at home in this quarter of the archipelago, he is quite an important personage. We hear that he was banished from the island where he was Rajah for heading an insurrection.

# CHAPTER X.

*At sea*, en route *for* TIMOR-LAUT, *9th July.*

IN the early evening of 6th July, we slowly
wound out of the harbour of Banda, leaning on
the rails to watch to the last the lovely verdure
of this mid-ocean speck. Turning from that
prospect, I found that the sea wore the peculiar
aspect which only three times in many months
of sailing I have witnessed. The water seemed
as if oil, sweeping in long, crestless, gently
undulating waves, while every colour in the
brilliant sunset sky was reflected with kaleidoscopic intermingling in the gliding mirror. Anything more soothing than to sit quietly and

watch the by-floating of such waves I cannot imagine.

Next morning we were up with the light to see the curious peaks of the east of Ceram, which slope down towards the many tiny islands of which Gessir—our next point of call—is the most important and interesting. The forenoon was intensely hot, and we could only keep under the awning, looking out on the pleasing prospect and the beautiful sea, which wore the loveliest of greenish-blue hues. But during the afternoon a breeze, almost cold, made it possible to go on shore and see for ourselves this marvellous little island fair. Gessir is a mere horse-shoe-shaped, cocoanut-fringed coral attol, once one of the most dreaded nests and secure hiding-places of pirates in these seas, but now one of the busiest and most curious marts in the extreme East, crowded with the representatives and the handi-work of every race in the archipelago.

It is the rendezvous of the paradise and other bird-skin collectors from the mainland of New Guinea, from Salwatty, Mysore, and Halmaheira, and of the pearl-divers of Aru ; hither the tripang, tortoise-shell, bee's-wax, nutmegs, dammar, and other rich produce from a multitude of islands are brought to be exchanged with the Malay and Chinese traders of Macassar, Singapore, and Ternate—for the scarlet, blue, and white cottons and calicoes of the Dutch and English looms, for the yellow-handled hoop-iron knives, which form the universal small change of these regions, and for beads, glass balls, knobs of amber, old keys, scraps of iron, and worthless but gaudy Brummagem manufactures. At certain seasons it is quite a rich zoological garden. Here may often be seen in captivity birds of paradise of species never yet seen alive anywhere else out of their own lands, parrots, lories, cockatoos, crowned pigeons, cassowaries, tree-kangaroos, and other animals which have managed to survive a journey thus far, but rarely farther west.

Leaving the same evening, on the 8th we steamed up the inlet which almost cuts off the head of New Guinea, save for a narrow neck of about five miles, between high lands on either shore, under which a procession of curiously shaped, abrupt-sided inlets ran as far as we sailed. The natural features of Macluer Bay are perhaps the most striking of any I have yet witnessed.

We lay about three miles off from the village, from which cargo was to be taken in, and as soon as we had anchored the natives crowded

round the vessel in their narrow prahus, trying
to sell fruit, fish, birds, mats, &c., while the
officers of the ship tried to exchange their cast-
off garments for the curious bows and arrows
of native manufacture, their weapons of war and
the chase. It was most amusing to see the
natives examining the old coats and trousers,
holding them up to the light to find holes and
stains : when the garment was very bad it was
rejected in disgust. And to see the captious
purchasers ! As if a few holes mattered !

About 4 P.M., while it was still intensely hot,
making me very grateful for the shade of an immense blue umbrella which the old Rajah gal-
lantly held over me, we went on shore, in one of
the ship's boats, to make our first acquaintance
with Papuans in their own land. We drew near
to some rickety-looking dwellings, on a platform
projecting about fifty yards into the sea, the
supports of which were so slight, and the spars
so open and fragile, that I should have thought
a dovecot insecure thereon, and was only reas-
sured when I reasoned that the pile of bags of
wild nutmegs lying on the edge, ready to be
transported to the ship, had been carried over it.
The only staircase was three bamboo-sticks, very
wide apart, and, moreover, so polished by naked

feet that with my boots I could obtain no hold. However, with a push from those in the boat, and a pull from H. above, I sprang up, and stood in a New Guinean village, their first white female visitor.

We were met by the chief, a middle-aged man, of anything but regal appearance, who wore for the occasion a faded silk *sarong* and some rude jewellery—doubtless come by through the Arabs, who stood by watching the despatch of the nutmegs, to collect which they had passed months in this rude savage life.

Greetings and salaams over, the Rajah's wife ran forward, and, a fold of her garment over each hand, took mine between, and dragged me, still running, into her dwelling. Here others joined us, and in similar fashion took my hand between their covered hands, which they then drew slowly over their faces, meanwhile bowing low. For a moment I was afraid, they pressed so close and were so excited ; but I could soon see that they meant only kindness. I took time to look round their dwelling, in which there was no attempt at furniture. A few rude vessels lay on the floor ; and some ashes in a corner showed that they made fire, and were thus far above the brute creation.

When they had duly examined me, I got out
of the hut, and passed over the platform to the
shore, taking care not to fall through the frequent holes; for though to a Papuan an accidental plunge into the sea is no disagreeable
diversion, to me it would have been a serious
discomfiture. Though the shore widens a little
way to the left, and leads by gentle slopes to
mountain heights, all that was between the platform and high perpendicular cliffs was a few
yards of ledges of rock, covered by a thin soil.
This seemed the village graveyard; for all about
were mounds, railed round with short stakes,
while some were quite curtained in with red and
white cloth.

While we inquired about these mounds through
the old pilot, the crowd had gathered, and I found
myself so hedged in that I could not move farther.
With a certain diffidence, looking first to see if I
would allow it, they gently pushed back my hat
to look at my hair, drew back my sleeves, lifted
my skirts, and laughed immoderately at my
boots. Presently, with shrieks of excitement,
the crowd parted, and, with no regard for her
evident shyness, a tall albino woman was dragged
forward by two others and shown to me as a sister! She was the only one who wore a white

garment (at least it had once been white), and was a marked contrast to the others, not only from her fair skin, but from her unusual height, and especially from her *coiffure*, which was quite remarkable. The hair was very fair, golden-tinged, and had the appearance of being carefully dressed, though it was nature which laid those rows of soft curls so neatly on her head. Her skin was as ugly as her hair was pretty, being of a reddish-yellow hue, as if raw from the sun; and her teeth, quite blackened, and filed almost to the gums, gave her anything but a prepossessing look.

I was glad when H. called to me that the boat could not longer wait, for the light would soon be gone. Turning, as I hastened away, to see the brilliant sunset, I was arrested, thinking for a moment that I looked on a black statue. Between me and the light, the better to see us, a lad had climbed on to a high ledge, close against the luxurious overhanging foliage — all lit up from the dying glow — of the precipitous rock, and, wearing only a red loin-cloth on his shining dusky skin, stretched forward in eagerness, quite unconscious of his graceful poise. He formed a picture of savage beauty which flashed indelibly into my memory.

The crowd followed us to the boat, and shout-
ed and waved in exuberant Papuan style as we
sailed away; while the Arabs, incongruous amid
their surroundings — gay for the day in long
white flowing robes, broidered vests, and bright-
coloured turbans—stood on the very edge, watching us as far as they could see us, with evident
sadness that their short intercourse with the
outer world had already ended. What a powerful incentive is his religion to an Arab, that he
can so separate himself from the amenities of
civilisation, and dwell for years among such
savages, gathering the products that will bring
him the means of accomplishing that visit to
the Sacred Tomb which will ensure his eternal
happiness !

Next day we sought to call at two villages
farther south; but in the night a squall had
come on, and during the whole day we had a
strong breeze and driving rain. At the first village no boat attempted to come off; at the second
some half-dozen tried to approach, but the waves
made such sport with their frail skiffs that it was
impossible to conduct any transfer. The rowers
were mostly women, much tattooed on breasts
and arms, who shrieked wildly, and in some cases
even dropped their oars in terror, when our ship

set off, and the turning of the screw added foam and spray to the already tempestuous sea.

We were glad when, on the morning of the 10th, we lay close into Little Ké Island—for we had both been quite sick and miserable in the rough weather. As usual, we were immediately boarded by the natives, and a repetition of the scene depicted by Mr Wallace with such absolute fidelity was enacted. I use his words, for I could not tell it better : " Had I been blind, I could have been certain that these islanders were not Malays. . . . These Ké men came up singing and shouting, dipping their paddles deep in the water and throwing up clouds of spray; as they approached nearer, they stood up in their canoes and increased their noise and gesticulations, and on coming alongside, without asking leave and without a moment's hesitation, the greater part of them scrambled up on our deck, just as if they were come to take possession of a captured vessel. Then commenced a scene of indescribable confusion. These forty black, naked, mop-headed savages seemed intoxicated with joy and excitement. Not one of them could remain still for a moment. Every individual of our crew was in turn surrounded and examined, asked for tobacco or arrack, grinned at and de-

serted for another. A few presents of tobacco
made their eyes glisten; they would express
their satisfaction by grins and shouts, by roll-
ing on deck, or by a headlong leap overboard.
Schoolboys on an unexpected holiday, Irishmen
at a fair, or midshipmen on shore, would give
but a faint idea of the exuberant animal enjoyment of these people." One quiet old man stood
over me in unpleasant proximity as I ate breakfast on deck; he seemed fascinated by the para-
phernalia of a civilised meal.

Of our short visit to Ké there is not much to
say. It is always interesting to us to learn the
characteristics of the people, to see their homes
and hear their speech. Numbers of the boats
for which the Ké islands are famous were moored
on the white beach—boats which, though built
without European tools, are as sound and close-
fitting as any made in our best shipyards. The
forests of Ké produce magnificent timber of various qualities, some of which are said to be superior to the best Indian teak. To make each pair
of planks used in the construction of the larger
boats, an entire tree is consumed. The sand on
the shore is the whitest I have ever seen. At
mid-day, when we were on shore, it hurt the
eyes so that we were glad to turn into the woods,

where the path leads among trees of immense height, giving perfect shade. We were accompanied by a number of men and boys, who evidently wished to make the most of their visitors. A post-holder had been established in Ké three months previous to our visit. He aided H. to purchase a native tombstone — a curious box which is set up on a pole, having the proportions and pretty much the appearance of a small dovecot. As we sailed out from among the low wooded islands, over which cloudlets of varied and fantastic shapes hovered in a soft-hued sunset, the dark hills of Great Ké filling in the horizon, we thought that Little Ké had a beauty of its own.

A night brought us to the Aru Islands; but we had to lie some distance off while the officers went in a boat to find out how far we might venture, for we had almost stranded. While we waited boats drew near, oared by curious-looking crews, who, we learnt, were the pearl-divers of Aru. I took them at first for women—a mistake due to their arrangement of the hair; for their immense mops of frizzy locks were gathered behind in a large chignon or knot, while the short escaped hair formed a fringe, the whole coiffure being an untidy copy of the fashion-

I

able style I had left behind in England. They crowded on board as soon as possible, and would not be deterred from coming on our deck, from which we begged they might not be banished. They walked about, examining everything with the interest and ways of children, and specially honoured us by their close attention—a liberty we could not well resent, since we were equally busy discussing them from top to toe. Tall athletic fellows they were without exception, and almost negro black. Besides the loin bandage of scarlet calico, they had narrow bands of finely plaited straw—on which beads, small shells, and tiny teeth of animals were sewn— on shoulders, wrists, calves, and ankles. The most sickening odour pervaded the air, probably from some sort of grease or oil with which they smear their bodies.

They lingered by the ship's side day and night during our stay. Their wide flat boats seem their homes, for a fire-place, some rude utensils for cooking, and sleeping-mats were to be seen in each; while elaborate carvings decorated both ends, which were crowned with bunches of casso- wary feathers. The pearl-diver's most treasured possession is evidently his box containing siri- leaves, betel-nut, and chalk, of which materials he forms a ball to chew. A leaf is selected from a store, a piece of betel-nut is laid on it, and a sprinkling of chalk is added; the whole is rolled together, and when masticated a brilliant scarlet juice emanates, which is squirted all over with evident pleasure. The box is really beautifully carved, and contains a smoothly sliding drawer, with compartments for the different articles. They seemed always to be chewing; for every time I looked over the ship's rail they were engaged in preparing the prized morsel, and with a delight which recalled the satisfied air of an old gentleman using his snuff-mull.

We went on shore early in the day, and found Dobbo a fair-sized village, wonderfully civilised-looking for this out-of-the-world corner. Chinese, Arabs, and Malays bustled in the chief street, where to almost half its breadth, in front of the shops, under great awnings of mattings, quantities of tripang or *bêche de mer* were being sewed into bags to ship with us; and piles of oyster-shells, in which the beautiful Aru pearls are found, were being arranged and counted for despatch to Europe. There they fetch a high price, and appear in our homes in the thousand forms of mother-of-pearl decorations which beautify our nick-nacks and adorn our persons.

Although pearls from the Sulu Archipelago are the finest in the world, of the six or eight leading varieties of shells brought to Europe, those from Aru are the most valuable. A diver will collect from twenty to forty shells a-day, according to the state of the sea, and from 130 to 150 tons are obtained annually from this locality. A single valve of the Aru shells weighs generally over a pound.

We went into several of the *tokos*, hoping to see some pearls and birds of paradise. But traders from Macassar had been recently in Dobbo, and had bought up almost all that was worth having, both of pearls and birds. So of the latter there were only one or two specimens of the commonest species, and of the former only one of any size, whose beauty and exquisite pear-shape made me envious of possession ; but I could have bought it cheaper in London.

We walked about a mile and a half beyond the village to visit a personage who has taken to himself the title of Rajah of Aru. He was a sailor in his youth ; but is now in his old age settled in Aru with superabundant wealth for life, with which he indulges in ludicrous and uncomfortable imitations of civilised luxuries. His house, originally a mere bamboo erection, was

almost covered with pieces of boxes—conspicu-
ously Huntley & Palmer's biscuit boxes, with the
bright labels still attached. A few dirty tattered
flags hung about; and as we approached, some
of the household bustled with preparation —
spreading a gaudy cloth on the table, coloured
covers on the chairs, and hanging pieces of red
and blue cloth here and there, so that the verandah was quite gay when we sat down. Numerous old rusty guns on primitive racks, and
about a dozen pistols neatly arranged, ornamented. the walls of the interior, which con-
tained a surprising collection of heterogeneous
articles stowed in corners and piled on shelves.

Being a Mohammedan, he had numerous wives,
who with a number of children peeped from the
doors of their apartments; but only one of his
wives, quite a girl, the mother of an infant
which he nursed with evident pride and many
caresses during the whole time we stayed, was
brought forward and introduced to us. Shortly
a Papuan slave, with her wild mop all unbound,
brought us *café noir*, kneeling as she offered it;
but fond as I am of this beverage, and tired out
as I was from the hot walk, I could not bring
myself to drink from the dirty-looking cups,
which were in keeping with the whole service.

Towards evening, while we were still resting on deck, the sound of tom-toms and gongs attracted our attention, and looking over the sea we saw a large prahu, oared by thirty rowers, approaching, most gaily decorated with branches and flowers. In the centre, under a great umbrella held by attendants, sat an old man, who shortly came on deck accompanied by four courtiers. I could not refrain from laughing aloud at the ludicrous appearance of the group before us, but was soon checked when I saw their really sorrowful countenances. It was the Rajah of some place in the neighbourhood; his son had just been murdered, and seeing a great ship lying off, he had come to ask if any redress could be obtained. The old chief wore bright green trousers, a long black coat, and *over* this a *kabia* or native jacket of bright purple satin, with inch-wide gold-thread stripes, and a very dirty and starchless collar lay untidily on his neck. Another had trousers of bright scarlet, with large butterfly pattern, a faded green silk coat brocaded with large gold flowers, and a shabby grey felt hat; and another a long surtout coat, with a much worn black satin vest, wrong side out, over it. Two others were not so abundantly clothed, for one suit served them

both.  It had evidently descended to the present
wearers from some passing vessel where theatri-
cal entertainments had been whiling the tedium
of a voyage, for the coat had a blue tail and a
red, and the trousers one leg of green and the
other of yellow.  Somehow the man with the
trousers looked much better clad than the
man with the coat.  These garments formed
doubtless the entire wardrobe of the village,
accumulated during who knows how many
generations.

A cool breeze prevailed during our stay at
Aru, and on the afternoon of the second day a
tropical downpour fell, giving us another opportunity of witnessing what is always an amusing
scene.  The sailors take advantage of the occasion to enjoy a freshwater bath and wash their
clothes.  Perching ourselves on the roof of the
cabin, as the driest spot available, but where a
fine drizzle came through even double awnings,
we watched the busy and delighted company as
they made themselves a shower-bath by jumping up and seizing the edge of the awning, thus
bringing down upon themselves a copious deluge
of water.  They lustily rub the garments they
wear, thus at the same time cleansing both their
bodies and their garments.  All drenched and

laughing, they then run off to put on dry clothing and hang up their washing.

And now I must bid you adieu for some months. We are approaching the Tenimber Islands, and after parting from the vessel can have no communication with the outer world. In my next you shall know how we fared during the three months we spend among a people whose reputation is not very favourable.

# CHAPTER XI.

TENIMBER—LARAT STRAITS—RITABEL—THE POST-HOLDER—
CHOOSING A SITE FOR A HOUSE—BUILDING—OUR NEW
DWELLING—OUR TRADE—GOODS AT A DISCOUNT—OUR VISI-
TORS—A STATE OF WARFARE—A PALAVER AT WAITIDAL—
ESCAPE.

BY daylight on the 12th we were sailing straight
for the Tenimber or Timor-laut Islands, through
a rough sea and a cold damp atmosphere. When
the islands were first discovered, and the name
Timor-laut or Tenimber first applied, is not
known. Our first reliable information about
them is derived from Captain Owen Stanley,
who, in his ' Visits to the Islands in the Arafura
Sea,' says : " We sailed from Port Essington on
March 18, 1839. . . . Light airs prevented our
clearing the harbour till the morning of the
19th, and at 3 P.M. on the 20th we made the
land of Timor-laut. . . . At daylight on the
21st we made all sail to the northward, . . . and

anchored in eleven fathoms, sand and coral, three-quarters of a mile from the shore. On landing, the contrast to the Australian shores we had so recently sailed from was very striking. We left a land covered with the monotonous interminable forest of the eucalyptus or gum-tree, which, from the peculiar structure of its leaf, affords but little shelter from the tropical sun; shores fringed with impenetrable mangroves, . . . the natives black, the lowest in the scale of civilised life. . . . We landed on a beach, along which a luxuriant growth of cocoanut trees extended for more than a mile, under the shade of which were sheds neatly constructed of bamboo and thatched with palm-leaves, for the reception of their canoes. The natives who thronged the beach were of a light tawny colour, mostly fine athletic men, with an intelligent expression of countenance."

On the morning of the 13th we finished our final packing in much discomfort, for the ship rolled badly, and the cabin windows were closed (always a misery to me) against spray and rain. It cleared when we were passing Molu and Vordate, smaller neighbouring islands; and as we drew near to Larat the sun shone out brightly, that we might not land on our adventurous life

under too disheartening auspices! We eagerly
looked from the deck as we came closer and
closer to the indented coast, whose low foreshore
was covered with a thick forest of cocoa-nut
trees and dark-green mangrove thickets, and
which, though not uninviting, formed a marked
contrast to the rich vegetation we had left behind in the Eastern Archipelago. At last the
ship dropped anchor close by the village of
Ritabel, in the narrow straits between Larat and
the mainland. As soon as we had made fast,
boats put off from both shores, and in a few
minutes we were surrounded by a little fleet,
whose occupants scrambled on board, talking in
exuberant Papuan fashion, affording us an opportunity of forming some opinion of our companions of the next three months. They were
powerful, athletic fellows, having rich chocolate-
coloured skins and flowing manes of gold-hued
hair, which gave them a most prepossessing air.
Two solemn-looking old personages—evidently
chiefs of their villages, for one wore a battered
grey hat, and the other a jacket of dark gauze
stuff, tied by the arms round his neck — kept
close to our elbow, and every now and again
making the action of raising a cup to the lips
and drinking, repeated "*laru*," the word for

gin. Having stilled their importunity by a
glass to each, we were besieged by the crowd,
and were glad to descend into the boats to go
on shore. A number of women stood close to
a shed on the beach, too shy to come forward,
but too curious to stay in the village. On coming quite near I was much disappointed in their
appearance, with their untidy mops and dingy
*sarongs*, for I had looked for handsomer help-
meets to the men.

Our fellow-passengers and the officers of the
ship accompanied us on shore, and went with
us into the post-holder's house. It was soon
arranged that we should rent a room from him
till we could get a house, and our baggage was
at once stored in his verandah. Within the last
few months the Dutch had asserted their rights
in some of these most outlying islands of their
possessions, and a post-holder is an official who,
by residence amongst the savage inhabitants,
upholds the authority of the Government, and
meanwhile impresses on the natives the benefits
of civilisation. Post-holders are themselves natives of the adjacent civilised islands, and besides the good education enjoyed in such, they
are specially trained for their post. A man of
natural energy and tact has great scope for his

powers, and can soon make his presence felt on the savage. This man and his household were left in Larat only three months previously, and you can imagine how eagerly we listened to their account of how they had established themselves. He himself, his wife, his young child, two policemen, their wives, and two hunters of the Resident, had to take up quarters in a shed on the shore which had served as village tap-room, and was only grudgingly conceded. Soon tempestuous weather came, and waves washed through the shed, drenching them as they lay, already prostrate from fever. The natives freely came and went, amusing themselves by looking on, but they either could not or would not understand their earnest request for water, so it was the work of the one of the party least feverish for the day to go to the distant well. The indifference of the savages was not from dislike; they had simply no idea of helping a fellow-creature.

The immigrants had had a great trial of patience in the erection of the house in which we sat, then, after three months' residence, not yet finished. Encouraging for us, who had no authority to insist on service, no flag to set up in token of power! When our friends of the ship

rose to go we accompanied them to the shore,
summoning all our courage to bid them a cheer-
ful good-bye ; and when the Amboina hoisted her
anchor and bore away, we sat down on a chest,
and watched her grow less and less and disappear over the horizon with feelings somewhat of
desolation, and not without misgivings, left as we
were without the possibility of communicating
with civilisation for at least three months to come.

Our first thought was for our house. When
the sun was declining in the afternoon, we set
off to look for a site. We had to pass through
the village, which is formed of irregular streets,
most of the houses having the gable to the sea
to allow of the prahus being run up under them.
The village is encircled by a high double palisade, and at the landward gateway, excepting a
narrow footpath, the ground is covered with
sharpened bamboo spikes. The villagers who
accompanied us pointed to these in the most
excited manner, warning us to beware of them,
and at the same time opening our eyes to the
fact that we were environed by enemies, and
that the village was standing on its defence.
Outside the gate we entered a cocoa-nut forest,
where, on the left, a high cliff stands, whose face
is almost hid with bunches of ferns and bright-

coloured shrubs, while graceful creepers interlace among the tall trees at its base and depend from its ledges. This is one of the prettiest little bits about us, and I was curious to get into the labyrinth to see its beauties nearer, while H. was as anxious to secure the large and beautiful butterflies which flitted among the bushes; but we dared not go near for the hidden bamboo spikes, which were thickly set just in this corner. There was no use building here, without the defences: we turned along the beach by a narrow stretch of sand, and then past a rocky piece of shore which is quite impassable at every full tide and shuts off communication from the next baylet, above whose sandy shore a few huts stand. From these about twenty men were turning homeward to the village, beyond which they do not linger after sunset, and they with the most earnest insistence tried to hinder us from going farther. We would not heed them, but kept on, and climbed the bluff, on which stands the half-burned and recently deserted village of Ridol. Here we were made alive to the reality of the warfare with other tribes, when we saw a human arm hanging from a branch of a high tree, and around recently gibbeted heads and limbs. How disappointed I was to have to

conclude that it would be unsafe to live anywhere but in the village. We turned back and
overtook the company who had tried to deter
us from going farther, under whose escort we
walked back to the village. I often recall my
impressions of that hour with pleasure. You
see us on the sea-beach at sundown,—would
that I could fill in the picture so that you could
distinctly imagine the group accompanying us,
and see the savage at home. Twenty lithe,
handsome young fellows, their golden manes
bound—some with scarlet cloth and some with
yellow leaves—with bright feather or gay flower
decorations stuck at the side and floating on
their dark brown skins, capering round, waving
their bows and arrows in the air, and brandishing their spears, and now and again drawing
near to examine our clothes and touch our hands
and faces. One spied the corner of H.'s red-
bordered handkerchief, and on being shown its
use the excitement became yet greater, and
they whooped and yelled in their merriment
like great children. One who had great preten-
sions to superiority on the strength of his having been away some months in another island,
and picked up some Malay, as well as a jacket,
which he wore sometimes in the usual manner

and sometimes as a turban, came quietly to my side, and as he rolled betel and chalk in the siri-leaf to place in his cheek, he begged me not to be angry—chewing siri and betel-nut was an old, old custom of the Tenimber people. Then he became confidential, and pointed out a great stalwart fellow who had lately killed one of the enemy, and asked me if I was not honoured to be in the company of a brave!

Next morning H. set about trying to get a site for our house fixed upon. We had now to learn that we might only have a house where we were permitted; for some days it was even under debate whether we might build there at all. They said, "There was the post-holder's party settled amongst them, and now we, more strangers, wanted to gain a hold in their village; they would rather be Tenimber people and keep to their own old ways."

We then proposed to go to the village on the other side of the strait, and H. went over to negotiate the matter. For three days the debate went on, now with exorbitant demands which would have made a hopeless gap in our store of barter goods, then with a doubt whether we should be received; but finally we were point-blank refused permission to build there. By

K

very liberal presents to the old men of Ritabel,
they were at last cajoled into allowing a site
just within the tide - mark, and close by the
stockade, on condition that they were not to
be troubled with the building of it; then only,
on the ninth day after our arrival, was our house
commenced. During the ten days until it was
finished we mingled much with the natives,
who were constant onlookers, and were at last
tempted by rewards to give some help, but
their efforts were very desultory. It may seem
a light matter to land on a savage island and
install one's self; but as I re-read my journal I
recall vividly the vexation of the delay, and the
constant restraint of our feelings lest we should
irritate the natives—for our progress during our
whole stay depended on the amicability of our
first relations with them. It was then I first
saw H.'s patience and tact displayed, when he
was chafing sorely at the waste of precious time
until he could commence the work he came
to do.

On the nineteenth day after our arrival we
were settled in our dwelling. It is raised a few
feet from the ground (for at high tide the waves
wash right under it), and contains two apartments,—a sleeping chamber, which is also writ-

ing-room, and a large outer room, which is dining-hall and general store. The men's apartments, the kitchen, and the drying-house, are
all close by. Although the walls are open
enough to admit plenty of light, we have two
windows, one at each end, both affording pretty
outlooks, but so high that I have to mount on
a box to see out. While with the post-holder,
we found that when the door was barred the
window was filled with eager faces, and we
thought by thus raising them to secure greater
privacy; but we find that every crevice in the
walls of our little room is held by a peering eye
as we sit writing by lamplight.

The days spent in waiting were not lost. The
post-holder is a dreamy sort of man, but his
wife is a wonderful little woman, full of energy
and tact. I always stood by her to learn as she
bartered for the day's supplies. The natives
pressed round with fish, fowls, yams, Indian
corn, bananas, melons; and though I could not
imitate her ways, I admired how well she kept
order in the unruly crowd, with loud good-
natured scolding, a push, a hearty slap, or a
kindly pat.

Our trade goods we find are for the most part
useless. Our beads they will not look at, they

are too coarse and large. In vain I have made
tempting strings of our gorgeous stock, which
would have gladdened the heart of any child at
home, and presented them to the little ones,
thinking to educate the taste to our wares, but
they would have none of them; their taste lies
in small red and blue sorts. Our German knives
and coloured calicoes are acceptable; a large
stock of white calico and various sizes of brass
wire were long rejected, but now later on are
more useful. I am amused to have to make
mention of some dimly printed sheets of calico,
which a trader in Banda solemnly assured us
were eagerly sought as grave-cloths. No Tenimber man ever saw such a shroud, and we are
unable to arouse any desire for the glory of such
a last wrapping. Arabs from Macassar come
every year to collect tortoise-shell in these parts;
but their trade must be among more civilised
people, with more wants, for such things as
matches, papers for cigarettes, and drinking-
glasses, which they recommended to us, we cannot dispose of in Tenimber.

The post-holder's wife manages to have an
excellent table from the few native products, and
we know the difference when left to the tender
mercies of Kobez, our own cook, who has pro-

fited little from the opportunity he had of learning in her kitchen.

Two privileged persons—the old Orang-kaya or chief of the village, and Borie, the man with the jacket, who knows a little Malay—are permitted to come into the house when the lamp is lighted and the door barred against the crowd. Borie is thus favoured that he may be questioned about the customs, laws, and history, past and present, of his people. He is a striking-looking and handsome savage, but I cannot quite like Borie. He can be such a sycophant when there is any hope of gin, and he has a cunning expression which makes me fight shy of any friendliness. The old Orang-kaya is an abject specimen of humanity. He sits—I mean crouches, none of them ever sit—gazing on us so meekly while the voluble Borie discourses. The poor fellow has had his house burned in a recent fray and lost all he had, and his wife was picked off from the palisade by a lurking Kaleobar marksman. The Tenimber men always have a ball of tobacco between the teeth and lips, causing the latter to protrude greatly; ordinary speech is conducted without disturbing this obstruction. The utterance is thus rendered thick and indistinct; but in animated discussion the ball is removed and tucked behind the ear, or carefully inserted in some crevice of the wall. I often poke out from the wall numbers of these balls, left by persons who have come to give information or bring some object to exchange, and gone off too engrossed in the reward to remember their uncoveted possessions.

A state of war exists between the villages of Ridol, Waitidal, and Ritabel (our village) on the one hand, and Kaleobar (one of the largest villages on the island), Kelaan, and Lamdesar on the other. Many of the villagers show us recent wounds received in a raid made a few weeks before our arrival. The bamboo spikes in the ground round the village were set to prevent such clandestine attacks. During the day they are removed from the paths which lead to the fields and wells; it is the duty of the first outgoer in the morning to open the gate and remove the spikes. At sunset, when the last man has returned to the village, the pathway is carefully reset, and the gateway barricaded for the night.

As the daily dread of attack by the Kaleobar tribes on our village has restricted operations to a narrow area, and kept us in a constant state of suspense and anxiety, H. proposed to the post-holder that they should together visit that village to try what could be done by personal influence to establish friendly relations. A chief from Sera, an island on the west coast, who speaks Malay, being on a visit to our village, agreed to accompany and promised to be hostage if they tried to detain H. I was miserably anxious while this was being proposed, and was cowardly enough to be glad when the postholder refused to risk his life in such an attempt, excusing himself on the plea that our neighbours of the next village, who had suffered badly in the last fray, would oppose a peace. H., however, determined to sound them, so anxious was he to have the range of the island, and be able to assure our men, who would hardly go to the well for water, and refused to proceed any distance into the forests to the hunt, that they might work without fear. How he fared, and how nearly I was left in the first fortnight of our stay to face the trials of such a life alone, I let H. tell in his own words :—

"As, like most of the Tenimberese villages, Waitidal was situated on a flat space of some extent on the summit of a bluff which stood a good way back from shore, we had, in order to reach the gateway, to ascend the perpendicular

face of the cliff by a steep wooden trap-stair,
which I observed was of dark redwood, its sides
elaborately sculptured with alligators and lizards, and surmounted by a carved head on each
side. On entering I saluted those near the
gate, but we were rather coldly received. As we
proceeded up the centre of the village, two
elderly men, evidently intoxicated, rushed at us
with poised spears, gesticulating and shouting
to those around to oppose us. The tumult
brought out the Orang-kaya, whose approach
prevented any immediate act of hostility, and to
him my guide explained the object of our visit.
Having shaken hands with us—a sign of friendship—he, accompanied by the older men, conducted us to his house, through the door-hole of
which I ascended with the uneasy feeling of
entering a trap. My proposals being fully explained to them, they were received at first
with little opposition, till my intoxicated friends
joined the circle. One was evidently a man of
some importance in the village, and at once
opposed the project in a spirit of hostility, which
gradually spread to the others. As no palaver
is ever conducted without profuse libations, raw
palm-spirit, distilled by themselves, was passed
round in cocoa-nut shell-cups, and I was expected

to keep pace—no slow one—with their drinking.
As the spirit circulated, the hostile feeling developed, especially as the discussion had merged
into another—viz., that I should be persuaded
to leave Ritabel and dwell in Waitidal. They
found I had sold much cloth and knives in Ritabel, but had brought none over to them : I could
have plenty of fowls among them ; they would
find me no end of birds, and would not cheat
me in the way the Ritabel people were doing.
To this, of course, I could not agree, and put
my refusal as pleasantly as I could. I tried to
bring the palaver to a close by rising to leave ;
but this they would not permit, for one of them
barred my exit by sitting on guard on the margin of the hatch. I shortly discovered that the
subject of their excited wrangling was whether
I should be permitted to leave at all. My guide,
after whispering to me not to be alarmed, and
adding a remark I did not comprehend, went
away, luckily leaving the door open, intending,
as I imagined, to return soon ; but he either
joined some other drinking-party and forgot to
do so, or purposely left me to my own resources.
Pretending to be quite pleased to prolong my
visit, I presented my cup for more spirit, and as
successive rounds were filled my companions

became incapable of observing that I did not drain my cup till I had passed its contents through the floor, and was imperceptibly nearing the now open trap-door. I took the first opportunity of diving through the orifice, and with a bold step shaped my course for the stairway at the top of the rock, where I felt I could dispute my departure on even terms. My guide appeared with rather a hang-dog look, and we wasted no time in getting to our boat and rowing out some distance from the shore."

## CHAPTER XII.

THE Ritabel villagers seem perfectly well-disposed towards us, and without fear or suspicion. I was soon welcomed among them, and am allowed to carry the babies,—good, interesting little creatures, profusely adorned with beads, and with their little limbs encased in a perfect buckler of shell bracelets : they wear a lighter shade of the chocolate skin which adorns their parents. I like to wander through the irregular paths intersecting the village, at sundown, when they are preparing the evening meal. Many of the mothers and maidens are stamping the Indian corn by the eaves, the fathers carry the infants, the young men dance on the shore, and the shout of the children at play rings through the village.

Their houses are very neat structures, elevated four or five feet above the ground, and entered by a stair through a trap-door cut in the floor, which is shut down and bolted at night. But domestic work could not be performed within them, for they are nothing more than floor and roof, so it is that they do everything *under* their dwellings.    There are, however, two fireplaces inside,—one for cooking when the weather is too boisterous out-of-doors, while the other is, as it were, nurse to the infants.    Coming home from a ramble one evening, ended by a stroll through the village, we were attracted to a hut where an unusual stir and brightness centred. They allowed me to climb up the trap-stair to see a newly-born infant, who was lying in a rude cradle (called in Tenimber language a *siwela*) of rattan wickerwork, with only a palm spathe beneath its back, and quite naked but for a tiny rag on its stomach.    But it was kept warm, as well as defended from tormenting mosquitoes, by being swung over a fire, on this occasion in a smoke so dense that I was amazed it was not suffocated.    To our utter astonishment we learnt that all quite young children are thus swung over the fire in the night, the mother having the end of a rope attached in her resting-place, and when the child screams she pulls the cord to rock it to sleep again. Sometimes the fire blazes up and burns out the bottom of the cradle; several severe accidents which had occurred in this way were related to us. I never saw children under about four months being carried about. They are allowed to lie in this hard cradle, always in the same position, flattening the back of their little heads till the deformity is quite pronounced and lifelong.

*30th Sept., at sea.*

I was quite unable to continue writing to you while in Ritabel: to keep my journal taxed all the strength which almost constant fever left me. We are now on our way back to Amboina, and I must make an effort to have this letter ready to post on arrival there, some ten days hence. I never seemed to realise until we were really off what a risk of life we have run; indeed I did not know it, for H. carefully concealed from me the reason of his nightly watches for the last six weeks. He professed that he slept in a chair to be ready to give me assistance while so weak, but the Kaleobar people had sent a threat that they were coming to attack our village, and it was to wait for them he sat. A small boat was hired and kept tied to the end of our house, and Lopez was instructed to take me across the strait, out of the fray, should the attack have been made before the steamer came.  Of course I should have refused to go,—anxiety for the others would have been unbearable; but in realising what a narrow escape we have had, I could not sleep at all the first night after sailing. All our experience passed before my mind, and a sickening terror, which happily never disturbed me while in the scene of danger, excited me painfully.

But let me continue the account of our life there.

We were settled in our own dwelling before fever came upon us.  I was last to succumb, though I had been suffering from headache and great lassitude for some time; but I had far worse attacks than any one when fever developed.  I cannot bear to look at my journal— the disheartening record of almost continuous attacks depresses me.  For three weeks I had an attack with delirium every day, and was greatly weakened.  A month after I say—" Only beginning to care to look from the window.  It is so difficult to pick up strength again.  Food which one eats with hearty appetite when well, is unpalatable in sickness, and a tempting morsel such as one could wish is unobtainable." H. meanwhile had several sharp turns. He was really very ill when suffering from an attack, for his was accompanied by violent retching; but he rarely was down longer than one day at a time. It was most fortunate that we were never at the worst together,—one was always able to help the other a little. Our men suffered considerably too. Kobez, however, made the slightest feverishness a cloak for his laziness, and often would not cook for us when he was best able of any; while to wash he refused point - blank, saying it always made him ill. Karl we have not found very obliging, but Lopez is always equal to an emergency. One day he came back from the hunt, and found me alone in the house making an attempt to prepare some fish, for we had had no food cooked that day. He tried to rout out the lazy Kobez, but even his efforts failing, he carried off the fish to the kitchen, himself cooked them, and served dinner most creditably.

I have frequently mentioned the yellow locks of the men. They are dyed by a preparation of cocoa - nut ash and lime, a fresh application being required once in three or four days to keep the rich golden colour. Some have straight hair, some curly, and others frizzy, but all bind it with coloured kerchiefs, or, failing such, a strip of palm-leaf. The gay young beaux spend much time in arranging the hair; those to whom nature has given only straight locks use a crimping instrument. Just behind the post-holder's house stood a long unused prahu, in which rain-water had collected, and this was the village mirror. It was an unfailing amusement to me to watch the row of youths standing there in the morning, tying with utmost nicety, and apparently with great vanity, the different-coloured bandages, one just edging over the other to see that the well-combed locks were properly confined, and finish with some last co-quettish touches. The old men do not dye the hair; many even middle-aged are being per-suaded of the benefit of having it cut short, and I was constantly being besought for a loan of my scissors. One day I had been cutting a red star from a label to paste on a child's forehead, when some of the onlookers—such were rarely absent from our house—got possession of them. H. asked me to try to get some specimens of the hair, and I motioned to a man to let me cut a piece. In the most complacent manner he laid his head on my lap, for he expected I was to

complete the cutting of his hair. This I did not
understand, however, and when I had cut one
lock, I proceeded to roll it in a piece of paper to
hand to H. The man looked up, and, to my
surprise, begged it back. I persisted in keeping
it, when the man broke into piteous tears, while
the others got quite excited, evidently more
with fear than anger, and joined him in entreat-
ing me to return it, which I was finally forced
to do. It seems the Tenimberese have the same
superstitious dread which exists in some other
islands, of any part of the person remaining in
possession of another; in some places the nail-
parings are carefully buried. During my dismay at the tumult I had occasioned, the scissors
again got into their hands, and haircutting in
earnest commenced. A strong wind then pre-
vailing blew scraps all over the apartment, and,
not caring for such in my dining-room (especially
as there seemed no chance of securing any, since
the urchins scrambled over each other after every
shred), I induced them to go out of doors. We
followed, and, spreading my skirts, I managed
to conceal a few pieces which the wind scattered, and cover them with my foot in the
soft sand, both of us carefully noting with an
outward air of unconcern from whom that dark

L

curl came, or that straight piece, or that yellow lock.

We soon learnt to converse with the natives, for they took the liveliest interest in all our doings, and accompanied us in all our walks. Perceiving that we desired to learn the name of everything we encountered, they themselves adopted the *rôle* of teacher, repeating to us their word for every tangible object, as well as trying to bring us to a comprehension of their expressions for abstract ideas. These savages cannot be indifferent to the beauties of nature. The talk of parent and child, as they walk in forest or by shore, or sail on the sea, must be of her wonderful works, for the very young children could tell the name of every bird, butterfly, tree, seed, flower, and shell. I recall with pleasure, though sometimes deafened by the clamour at the time, how they used to pull my skirts and hold up some object, distinctly pronouncing its name. After some days our friends began to catechise us in past lessons, bringing us various objects whose names they had already given, and requiring us to repeat the word, laughing heartily when we made a failure or a mispronunciation. The buttons on our garments formed excellent objects on which to teach us numeration, and

certain villagers would never let us pass, on en-
countering them, without hearing the unforget-
able *esā, eroo, eteloo, efāt, elima, enean, efitoo,*—
one, two, three, &c.

We were rather pestered by their perpetual
presence in our dwelling, for, like all untutored
races, their inquisitiveness knows no bounds.
From morning till night we had constant relays
lying in, or sitting about, our house, whom it
was impossible to dismiss without giving offence.
One day the hunters brought in a snake, already
dead, but at the sight of it all near fled in the
wildest terror.    This hint H. made good use
of, and when we were not in the mood to be
interested watching their ways, or found them
objectionable at meal-times, H. would cautiously
insert his hand into the large tin where his
specimens were kept in spirit, without any apparent reference to our visitors.    Of course they
pressed round to see what was going on, but
when he withdrew his hand with a writhing
snake in it, they would tumble over each other
out at the door, screaming and shouting.    As
they never waited to see how the matter ended,
they never came to know that we did not have a
mania for keeping live snakes.

We managed to make them understand that

our inner apartment must not be entered; at
the very first we would call out warningly when
any of them seemed about to venture in, and I
believe not one of them ever saw the interior.
During the weeks I was prostrate they were
quite annoyed, the post-holder said, that we
stayed so much indoors, and some of them stood
constantly by the window, which was too high,
however, for them to see in readily. Growing
impatient, they would call, " Non ! non ! nony !
Tuan ! tuan ! tuany ! "[1] the diminutive being
uttered in a most pleading and cajoling tone.
Having seen that H. wanted to buy objects of
ethnographical interest, they brought all sorts of
things, and held them up at the window. There
was no article in their possession, from a garment
to their own teeth, from their looms to their
necklaces, that was not persistently pressed upon
us ; and it having got abroad that H. wanted
skulls, they imagined that skulls and bones of
any kind would be equally acceptable, and
gathered from the refuse-heaps near the village
all they could find, offering them with such a
clamour that I was quite irritated in my weakness.

---

[1] *Tuan* is " master "; *nonya* (or *nony*, as they said it) is " mistress " or " lady."

The women, if not treated with a great show
of affection, and though left to perform all the
harder duties of life, are not subjected to restraint, and have a free and happy air about
them.  It is they who go to the distant forest
to cultivate on the poor soil covering the coral
rocks the sweet-potatoes, manioc, sugar-cane,
Indian corn, cotton, and tobacco which are needful in their daily life.  It is they who stamp the
Indian corn into meal; all day long, somewhere
in the village, the dull thud of the stamping-
pole in the large *tridacna* shell is heard.  They
must have good muscles; they lift the heavy
pole as if it were a bamboo.  And how deftly
they keep gathering in the grain with the left
hand, scarcely any being spilled from the shell
in the stamping.  What does fall is at once
picked up by the fowls, which are domestic pets;
and possibly from this food the Tenimber fowls
are in excellent condition, and particularly well-
flavoured.

Here and there a woman is to be seen sitting
close under the eaves of her house weaving cloth.
Her loom is indeed an heirloom, and the simple
contrivance is often elaborately carved, it being
the pastime of lovers of successive generations to
make fresh carving on the fair one's loom.  The

buckle of her waistband is also his work; I am
not quite sure but that it is a token of betrothal
when a girl wears the buckle her suitor has made.
One end of the loom is fastened to a strong pole
lying horizontally, against which the weaver
presses her feet, and the other end is held fast
by a band round her back; thus her work is
kept stretched, and I have stood hours watching
her lift the threads, and form—with, to me, deft
and bewildering swiftness, as well as surpassing
patience—the favourite Tenimber pattern which
borders all the garments they make.

Two kinds of cloth are made, one from beautiful soft cotton, grown by themselves, which,
with a curious little spindle or twister, and a
store in a tiny basket depending from the arm,
they form into thread, dyed afterwards blue and
scarlet, among which colours white is intermingled in the weaving. The result is a pretty
and very soft cloth, and it is worn by the women
when the evening chill comes on, but too often
it is taken in loan by the men.

The other material is used as a *sarong* or
petticoat, and is manufactured by a patient process from the leaves of a palm - tree. The
leaves are split into stripes of about an inch
wide, then the outer skin is peeled off by the

aid of a knife, after this they are divided into
many very fine threads, made into neat bundles,
and converted into one long thread by a series
of knots. Then the threads are dried and dyed,
and twisted by a spindle like that with which
the cotton is spun; they are then ready for
weaving. The cloth from these is rather hard,
and has a lustre. The colours used in this
material are black, yellow, and red: all their
dyes are made by themselves from barks and
roots. I believe no one ever attempts an inno-
vation of fashion. The scant *sarong* has been
the Tenimber woman's dress for who knows how
long,—how much longer will it be? Now that
civilisation has approached them, their life will
not long preserve its savage simplicity. Man-
chester looms will weave their *sarongs*, and
after-dwellers will not be able to see Tenimber
matrons, maidens, and the tiniest girls who can
hold a twister, busied in every spare moment as
they loiter by the doorway or trudge along with
their burden, spinning thread for their excellent
and durable petticoat.

A fashionable toilet would be quite lost on
them. One of the ship's company, who landed
with us when we came, left with the post-holder
a sheet from a French fashion journal, which

was hung on his wall. It represented ideal figures of ladies, in walking, riding, bathing, mountaineering, and gymnastic costumes : as far as I observed,—and I noted their manner carefully,—they saw no resemblance to human beings in these figures; they were as triangles or squares to them. Ah! may advancing civilisation keep such monstrosities far from the graceful Tenimber women. With head erect and chest expanded, how easy, graceful, healthy, happy they looked! Untrammelled in limb, free of foot, it was worth while to watch their every motion. As they came home in their prahus from their gardens over the strait, always just at sundown, when their figures, as they stand erect at the stern, show clearly against the ruddy light, with a powerful push of the pole, and an exquisite action of the body, sending the prahus shooting up the beach, they showed at their best, and formed a picture we never tired looking on.

There is no question that the beauty of the Tenimber women is in their healthiness and natural grace of movement—not, except in a few cases, in delicacy of feature. In budding womanhood some of them look sweet,—pensive eyes and the soft brown skin make up a pleasing face ; but later they get thin, and the skin becomes shrunken. They do not dye the hair as the men do, and give little time to its arrangement. I never heard a woman sing. They may, but I did not hear even the " li-li-la-a-a-a," which is the spontaneous expression of exuberance and content with the man, who also frequently bursts into wild happy song. They laugh often, however, with true Papuan heartiness. And they can scold too ! I once saw a woman rating her husband soundly ; he, however, took it very coolly, and went on quietly baling water from a prahu with a cocoa-nut, wisely letting her expend her wrath without a word. I was surprised at the violence of passion displayed once by a little girl of about six years of age. Her mother and friends were sailing from the shore, going evidently to a distant garden, and for some reason she had to be left behind. She ran into the water, screaming violently, and tried to clamber into the boat. Seeing this hopeless, she came back and threw herself on the sand, beating her feet and tearing her hair ; occasionally she would rise, run a little, and then fling herself down again. Her state seemed to excite no pity from the onlookers. I tried to divert her, but she seemed deaf and blind from grief.

Hours afterwards I saw her crouching in the village, sobbing gently still, and looking utterly exhausted from the outburst.

But this was a single instance. When I think of the little girls, I always see a more pleasing and peaceful picture. They sit for hours in the required posture before tiny looms, imitating their mothers weaving, with real, and sometimes only imaginary, shuttle and warp. At a very early age they commence to carry burdens as their mothers do. A child of eight years carries a weight on her back, held by a band round the forehead, which would make me stagger.

A man may have as many wives as he can purchase, but as a rule it is all he can do to secure one, at least till he is considerably advanced in years, and has disposed of some of his daughters for gold ear-rings and elephants' tusks, which are indispensable. These tusks are brought chiefly from Singapore and Sumatra, where they cost 200 or 300 florins each, by the Buginese traders, who with the westerly winds seek out the creeks and bays of the "far, far east" to exchange them for tripang and tortoise-shell. The father of the girl has often to wait a long time for the ivory portion of her price; but he hands her over, on the payment

of the other items of the bargain, to her purchaser, who takes up his abode in her house,
where she and her children remain as hostages
till the full price is paid. A girl sorely wounded
by the blind god occasionally takes the settlement of affairs into her own hands, and runs
away with the object of her affection, without
the permission of her parents — a proceeding
which does not relieve him of the purchase-
money. If, however, she had been or was about
to be disposed of to another man, and had eloped
with a more desired youth, she would be forcibly seized, and her companion punished with
death.

# CHAPTER XIII.

RITABEL——MEN——THEIR EMPLOYMENT——EATING——WAR-DANCES
——MORALS——BOYS——BABIES.

THE men have the advantage of the women in looks ; they give more time to personal decoration, and do not toil. They are undoubtedly lazy fellows, and seem to work only when in the mood. Their only regular task is the bringing of the *tuak* which has dropped into a bamboo attached high on the stem of the palm-trees, and this is performed by the young men just after the morning hairdressing. We have often stood in our morning stroll to watch the Tenimber athlete mount the tall bare stem, climbing the slight notches cut in the tree with regular, unfaltering step, and singing gaily the while, his faultless brown form and waving yellow hair showing clearly against the palm's soft grey in the oblique morning sun, till he was lost in the shadow of its feathery crown.

With kindly manner they would accede to
my wish to taste of the liquid they had just
brought down.  Seeing I shrank from drinking
from the rather dirty bamboo, and objected to
the insects which had dropped into it, the gal-
lant would make me a cup of a fresh green leaf,
and with a tiny bundle of dry grass form a
strainer.  The young men then join the elders,
when they repair in companies—whether composed of relations or merely on the ground of
friendship I cannot say—to large sheds in or
near the village, to partake of the chief meal of
the day.  They remain here cooking, eating,
and sleeping for many hours.  The older men
seldom end this meal sober, and cease only when
fairly incapable of further imbibition : not only
do they drink the very slightly fermented *tuak*
just brought from the trees, but also a distilla-
tion of it, made with a most primitive contrivance of a bamboo and a gourd over a slow fire.
Therefore when they emerge from these huts
towards sundown they are querulous, and pug-
nacious and boisterous talking is occasionally
heard in the village.  The young men, if they
taste the *tuak*, do not take enough to be intoxicated, and come forth after their slumbers
through the heat of the day with all their

vigour to dance on the shore or practise the drawing of the bow and the throwing of the lance. This was a beautiful exhibition, and as I looked on I could well understand Mr Wallace's words—"Here I was delighted with the beauty of the human form, a beauty of which stay-at-home civilised people can scarcely have any conception. What are the finest Grecian statues to the living, moving men I saw around me? The unrestrained grace of the savage as he goes about his daily occupations, or lounges at his ease, must be seen to be understood; and a youth bending his bow is the perfection of manly beauty,"—and not less so, I would add, when throwing his lance. Pity the foe who met such a cast! Strong, and free of limb, practised in his art from his boyhood, the thrower would gather up his strength, concentrate all his energies, and rushing forward, send forth his spear like an arrow from a bow.

When war is threatened, at time of full moon the youths undertake to watch the common safety, and dance the *tjikelele* all night round a pole, which they say is Duadilah, their deity. Only in moonlight could the enemy see to make their way through the forest, and the villagers dance, shout, and beat their drums to let the foe hear that they are on the alert, as well as to keep themselves awake. Although it was sometimes distressing, when suffering from actual fever or the weakness it left behind, to have this perpetual clamour so near to one, we should have been duly thankful to our guardians had they only given up when daylight rendered further effort needless. They generally danced from sundown till ten next morning, but sometimes they seemed to get intoxicated with excitement and to be unable to stop, and we had days and nights of unceasing noise.

Although so exciting to themselves, their dance is rather uninteresting to an onlooker after having once seen it. Eight or ten, each with a cylindrical drum in his hand, form a circle, and commence a slow swaying motion, changing gently from one foot to the other with each stroke of the drum, while maintaining a crouching attitude which does not show the figure to the best advantage by any means. One, meanwhile, in a sing - song monotonous voice, asks fowls to eat, *saguire* to drink, success in war, immunity from sickness, the wife he wants, and any particular need. At a certain point the others join in loud chorus, the beat of the tom-tom quickens, the gentle swaying

changes into stamping, the company draws closer
to the centre, and intense excitement prevails
as they come to a climax with wild yells and
shouts, bounding leaps in the air, and powerful
strokes on the drums. In the sudden silence
which succeeds, another voice in rotation takes
up the tale: it seems to me that when they
have gone on for hours, and exhausted every
rational request, they get imaginative, and, like
boys telling wonderful tales, each tries to outdo
his fellow in the extravagance of his impromptu
invocation. At this dance they wear all their
ornaments, such as large and heavy carved
combs, necklaces which dangle on the breast,
and ear-rings.

It was frequently a subject of discussion between H. and me whether this was the only
dance of the people. Towards the end of our
stay a young man was very anxious to be possessed of a gay red-and-yellow handkerchief we
had, such as his companion, the chief's son, was
wearing with great pride. But he never brought
us anything to barter of nearly sufficient value
for it, and as our stock of goods was getting low,
we could not afford to be as generous as I was
tempted to be, for he was a comely youth with
a pleasant face, and the most enviable crown of

golden curls, which deserved a pretty kerchief to bind them. He said he would dance for the kerchief, but we, not knowing we were to see anything new, would only come to terms for six feet of brass wire. He then commenced what is, I suppose, the Tenimber Highland fling, and for about a quarter of an hour kept up a succession of lively steps, ending with some difficult movements as agile as graceful. Quite breathless, he then came forward for his reward. Need I say he received the coveted handkerchief, and had I known the expressions in Tenimber, I should have offered profound thanks for the treat. This dance is altogether different from the *tjikelele*, but the same crouching attitude is maintained. This must be thought desirable by them : some grotesque figures we bought represented men dancing in this position. I was surprised at the accurateness of the copy, but undoubtedly their artistic ability is very high. They are deft-fingered and clever carvers of wood and ivory. The figureheads of their outrigger prahus, dug out of single trees, especially attract attention by the excellence of the workmanship, carefully and patiently executed, and the elegance of their furnishings; while the whole length of the central pillars of their houses is also most elaborately

M

carved with intricate patterns and representa-
tions of crocodiles and other animals.  Their
appreciation of beauty is a characteristic of them,
which, absolutely wanting in the Malay people,
I was surprised to find among a less advanced
race.  While walking through the forest they
invariably pluck and tastefully arrange in a
hole in their comb, which is there for the very
purpose, any particularly bright bunch of flowers.

A word of their morals, before I tell you of my
friends the boys.  These are such as might be
expected from a rude people subjected to no restraint.  Where they think they can escape
detection, they lie and steal without compunc-
tion, though their laws punish the latter offence
with slavery, from which the thief can be ran-
somed only by a great sum.  To their enemies
they are savagely cruel, executing on those that
fall into their hands the most revolting atrocities
before affixing their dismembered quarters to
their public places.  They are essentially selfish,
and devoid of all feelings of gratitude or pity.
To give anything for nothing would be a breach
of all hereditary instincts.  In their cups they
are easily offended, and in all cases one has to be
very wary in dealing with them, for the true
savage comes out when they are roused.  We

had once to hide our man Carl for three days in our room. A man supposed (wrongly) that Carl said he stole a knife, and he waited by our door all that time with his spear ready. The matter was finally explained and the man pacified. One day Kobez, our cook, was washing : a few young men from another village were visiting our village of Ritabel, and being very curious regarding our house, which had been erected since their last visit, they were making themselves at home inside. Kobez deprived them of the pleasure of watching him by shutting the door, but they kept peering through the chinks, and making loud and eager remarks. I suppose Kobez was irritated, for he pitched a cupful of soapy water just where their eyes were. Of course, in any civilised country, one might throw water at one's will in the interior of a dwelling ; but these savages know no such niceties of law, and you should have heard the tumult ! We really expected to be attacked, and it was only after many hours that we felt out of danger. One morning the most appalling shrieking and moaning arrested our attention. Two men had quarrelled over a piece of cloth ; one had taken the other's child, and had a cord round its neck to hang it. There was he running with the child on his shoulder, and the whole village—man, woman, and child—in the fray. H. and the post-holder went into their midst and managed to quiet them.

Still, as a rule, when sober they are good-natured enough, and live in harmony with each other. They are a simple, bold, free people, ingenious and ingenuous, supplying their own every absolute need, utterly untaught in civilised ways. They know no rule, no master, they do not understand obeying; you may beg, bribe, barter, you need not command.

Now as to the boys—such nice little lads they are! When I first went, I used to play with them on the sands at sundown, running races, and taking an interest in their games; afterwards, when weakened by fever, I used to draw objects familiar to them on the sand, and they guessed what they were. I could then talk with them, and they seemed to enjoy the fun as much as I. How near of kin is the whole world! At a very early age the children begin to wade about the shallow margins of the sea, practising with spear and arrow the capture of fish, training arm and eye, till, when they have come of age, they have attained an almost unerring accuracy of aim. One of their great amusements is the sailing of little boats, which they enter for championship in spirited regattas. A tiny fellow can, from the soft sago-palm stem, himself shape and set with sail, and fit with rudder and oars, an excellent miniature of the prahu his father sails. They also build forts of sand, just like our boys at home, and defend them against their comrade foes with balls of wet mud, as our boys cannot always do. One tumble in the sea removes all trace of the fray from these little naked savages, while no end of brushing would be necessary to clean little English boys' suits. The older lads, and sometimes the men, used to look on with much pleasure at this play, and the shout of laughter which hailed a good hit told their enjoyment and interest. The chief game is, however, one of more skill and precision, and although very little lads try it, the grown youths, and even the men, take part in it. It is played with discs cut off the top of the *conus* shell, and each player has two, one of which he places in a depression in the ground, and with the other he takes aim from a crease a few yards distant. Passing his right hand holding the disc round to his left side as far as he can stretch, and steadying it with his left, he takes aim with eager, glancing eye; then advancing with a run, he de-

livers with all his might. If he fails to hit, he
returns to the mark to play again in his turn;
but if he has succeeded, he plays a second time
from where his quoit rested. There is a great
similarity to marbles in this game, but marbles
are much more easily played than the discs.

Most boys from ten to twelve have frightful
sores upon the arms, produced by burning with
stones heated in the fire. We were told this is
to prevent small-pox, and they consider the scars
a sign of bravery : this is, as it were, their bap-
tism to the name of " brave." These sores must
give great pain indeed. Flies constantly settle
upon them, which they whisk off very cleverly
without apparently hurting the wound; but I
have sometimes seen them blowing on them,
and doubtless the brave little martyrs must
endure an amount of suffering of which a vaccination wound gives but a faint idea.

I must give a word to the babies now, and am
able to assure you that these savage parents are
never harsh with their infants. To see the
fathers carry them about in the evenings with
kindly care, one could scarcely believe in the
ferocity of their natures as we have sometimes
seen it exhibited. The mothers seemed pleased
at the notice I would take of their little ones,

who, like those with white skins, derive amusement from small dolls, stuffed with rice grains instead of sawdust. The packets of sugar I bestowed were inviolately kept for them, and given little by little, though evidently very tempting to the mothers themselves. The baby arms and legs are almost covered with circlets of shell, bone, and brass, with which the mother plays, rattling them up and down as she dandles the child; and almost all the beads and buttons they get hold of go to adorn the little necks. I do wish that the need of warmer coverings had suggested itself to their minds. I have often seen the infants shrinking from the evening wind, and am assured that they really suffered discomfort from the cold.

We are now drawing close to Amboina, having returned by the exact route by which we went. We were rather disappointed that we did not have the opportunity to go by the other, with which we are unfamiliar—*i.e.*, coasting the west of Timor-laut, touching at Sera, Babbar, Wetter, and thence returning to Banda and Amboina; but it really mattered little, as we were unable from weakness to go much on shore. We picked up wonderfully towards the end of the fortnight on shipboard, enjoying ease of mind, and an atmosphere free from malaria.

# CHAPTER XIV.

AMBOINA.

I AM writing in the house of Mrs Machik. Since we last saw them, they are established in a large dwelling looking out on the exercising plain, commanding a beautiful view of the bay and the hills beyond. But I shall finish my account of Tenimber before I tell you of the pleasure and beauty of life here.

We had frequently visitors from other villages. These seemed specially dressed for the occasion, the men having both head-dress and loin-cloth, ornamented with fancy stitches which would do credit to a deft needlewoman : patches and stripes of red, white, and blue are really tastefully intermingled on both articles of apparel, and beads form a fringe to finish the loin-cloth.

Ritabel villagers, too, have holiday garb, but it is rigorously kept for special occasions. Anything gay always goes on the head ; it is amusing to think that the considerable quantity of cloth we have given in barter has all gone to clothe that member, already so amply covered by the mass of frizzy hair. The men wear immense ear-rings of bone or ivory, so heavy that they often tear away the cartilage of the ear. The women have a graduated series of holes pierced all round the ear in girlhood, and until they can obtain the silver or gold rings they desire, the holes are kept open with points of thorns or tiny pieces of wood. Frequently they die without having ever had the number of rings to fill the holes, but at any rate they hoped to the last, for they were often to be seen readjusting the substitutes. Some also have toe-rings and anklets of brass, and there is no one that has not an armlet of some kind, of brass or ivory, or only of shell or wood. Both sexes tattoo a few simple devices on the breast, brow, cheek, and wrists, but never anything elaborate, such as the Papuans have whom we saw at the New Guinean ports we have just called at as we sailed north. The women think it a mark of beauty to have the teeth filed, and some have only a narrow black rim left protruding from the gums.

It was not so very hot in Timor-laut. It was not the cool season during our stay, for we had very little rain indeed, but there was often a strong breeze from the sea, which had this comfort that it carried off mosquitoes; but it was simply courting a fever attack to go out in it. It used to blow through the strait in a gentle hurricane at times, and then we were anxious for the boats crossing, which often barely escaped being carried out to sea. Occasionally there was a soft balmy wind, but it was even more deadly. I see by my journal that one such evening we strolled out by the shore, and stayed long watching the lizards and the hermit-crabs at their funny tricks; and the tide being back, we saw many varieties of shells. We sat down on a tree-stump to enjoy the scene before us,—the blue-green channel, the rich verdure-clad islands beyond, the soft blue and pink tinted sky overhead, mingling evermore in the rich sunset. Warned by this glow we loitered homewards, the golden lights on our faces and the soothing breeze lifting our hair, full of satisfaction and enjoyment. But, alas! the journal contains no further record till three weeks afterwards, when I resume, " I am for the first time able to write, having been day by day prostrated by fever."

Perhaps want of fresh water was one cause of our constant suffering. All our so-called fresh water was skimmed off the surface of holes made in the coral, and was brackish and unpalatable. There are no mountains in the islands, and no fresh-water streams. There was a spring in the village over the strait, but, as I have said, the boats could not always cross on account of the strong winds and currents. Then towards the end of our stay our villagers quarrelled with them, so that war was on the point of commencing, and our men would not venture across.

The natives are not unhealthy themselves. Occasionally they had fever, and the old had rheumatic limbs, but they seem to have excellent constitutions, and we never heard of any epidemic disease having appeared among them. I can recall one sickly lad. He looked about twenty, and was so thin; he never tried to join the sturdy merry lads of his own age, but stayed by a fire tending the smoking of pigs' flesh.

All immigrants, however, suffer greatly in acclimatising. Every one of the post-holder's party, who preceded us by three months, got sadly emaciated; his child died, and one woman seemed dying. Marcus, an Amboinese policeman, was a great boon amongst the men; he had such a merry heart, and was always able to influence them from his own exuberant spirits. But Marcus was not long of succumbing also to the depressing fever, and his attempts to dance, sing, and joke got rarer and rarer. Even the dogs were pitiable objects. They lost their hair and got thin too, and seemed scarcely able to drag their limbs along.

When we first went we were very well off for food. We took rice, coffee, tea, sugar, biscuits, and absolute necessities; and fowls, fish, fruit, and some vegetables we readily got. After about six weeks' stay, however, the fowls in our village were nearly all consumed; the natives had sufficient of our beads, cloths, &c., to be rather indifferent about more, so that they did not then care to go fishing with the set purpose of bringing food for us and exchanging it for some desired article; they did not cultivate more Indian corn and sweet potatoes than sufficient for their own needs, and as such are the staples of their food, they could not part with what they had, and we were often very badly off.

We purchased in Macassar twelve dozens of barter-knives for ten rupees, and for one knife we used to get a fowl, or more often two fowls

for three knives; a large fish, which was dinner
for the three men and ourselves, for two knives;
and ten eggs for one. But we were five, and
the post-holder's party nine, so in time the
supply was not equal to the demand. Kobez
often hunted half a day for a fowl, and we had
to give ten times as much as when we first came.
Kobez made this an excuse for the most trying
irregularity in serving our meals. I am sure he
just amused himself when he went seeking food.
Sometimes when he went over the strait, I could
see him sitting on the beach for hours, making
no effort to buy, and we famishing all the time
for breakfast. We had a cup of coffee on getting
up at 5.30,—that is, at daybreak. If you want to
have any enjoyment out of a tropical day, you
must get up then and go out in the morning
coolness and freshness. In our coffee we soaked
biscuits, made in Amboina of sago and canary
nut: they are like stones until soaked, but then
with considerable risk to the teeth you can manage to masticate them. The taste is very sweet
indeed; but though we had a large stock, they
were too difficult to eat to enjoy a satisfying
meal from them. At 10 we were supposed to
have breakfast, at which we had fowl or fish,
and rice or potatoes, with sago and cocoa-nut

milk as a pudding. When I was well punctuality was enforced, but later, when Kobez was left to himself, and when he had to hunt for food, he offered the meal at various hours, from 8 A.M. till 3 P.M. Shall I ever forget how I suffered from faintness for food in that place! In the afternoon we had a cup of tea, and should have dined at sundown, about 6.30. Sometimes we had that meal (the same viands as at breakfast) ready at 4 in the afternoon, and sometimes not till 10 P.M., when I was so sleepy and tired that I had gone to bed. Kobez seemed to have no power of reckoning time or arranging his work.

I think I have said that the fowls were of excellent quality, being reared chiefly on the grains of Indian corn spilled in stamping; but the fish were even more delicious. Indeed I have never anywhere seen such variety, or tasted such excellence. Fortunately we got very fond of having them cooked in cocoa-nut oil (which some people cannot taste); and I used to think we could never be badly off beside this teeming sea. But the natives would not go fishing for us when they had got surfeited with our goods. Occasionally they went out to take for themselves, and when we saw them

setting off, we had high hopes that perchance
we might persuade them to give us some of
their catch. We were sometimes not only disappointed but tantalised. A man brought once
to our door a large piece of a fish, with a bunch
of small ones of a particularly delicious flavour
attached. He wanted a button for the whole,
a bright gilt button, such as I had had on my
dress; but I had cut them off one by one at
different times, and had then no more of that
kind. I offered him a jacket of H.'s complete,
with bone buttons; he would have none of it,
nor anything in our whole stock. We bartered
long, for we really needed food. He sat by the
door till afternoon, thinking that at last I would
produce the coveted button; then he hung the
fish on a pole in front of our door, and went,
leaving them spoiling in the strong sun before
our eyes. Next morning we had to send for
him to remove them, stinking by that time.
We dared not have taken them : to have done
so would have probably cost us our lives.

You will wonder that we did not send our
own men to fish. Even if we had had the
necessary appliances, we dared not. The fishing-
ground of the natives is their most prized possession ; the commencement of their fierce and long

warfare with their Kaleobar foes was some dispute about the division. Fishing, the chase, and war, are the defined duties of the male sex, and they throw all their heart into these when they do engage in them. It is rather pretty to see them set off fishing. They choose the darkest nights, and at one end of the prahu a great bundle of prepared wood is ablaze to attract the fish. In this light one can clearly see their figures, as they busy themselves with preparations for their work, or stand poling the prahu along the coast in the graceful attitude so natural to them.

A few of them keep a single pig penned close by the dwelling, but there were never many in the village, and none were ever offered to us for sale. These pigs are wild, and are generally brought in when they go on the buffalo hunt. We were told that they sometimes bring back a buffalo, but such good fortune never happened while we were there.

About the middle of our stay our coffee went done. We gave of it to the men when down with fever, knowing ourselves the advantage of a hot drink during the terrible ague. Then we were thrown entirely on tea. Alas! that failed us too. Being so often sick, I did not have the same care of things as I should otherwise have had, and neglected to put it in the sun to prevent it spoiling in the tropical moisture. If we had been wise we should have had it in sealed tins; but it is H.'s way to be absolutely indifferent to personal comfort, and I was too inexperienced then in the housewifery of a tropical climate to be on the outlook. So it was almost all mouldy when we were warned to open the packages by discovering one quite white. Sorely grudging the necessity, we threw out all the bad packages, and the only consolation was that henceforth we had tea which could not harmfully affect the nerves!

Our salt, sugar, and soap held out to the last, and there remained considerable quantities of each to give to the delighted natives when we departed.

About the third day before we left a strange boat came, bringing some turtle-flesh. I believe they dry it in the sun and smoke it. What we got looked like sheets of glue, and we could not manage to eat it; but our men cooked it in some way, and seemed to enjoy it greatly.

Lopez and Carl, the hunters, went to the outlying islands of Molu and Maru to collect specimens of the birds and plants there. On their return, after ten days, they brought us a number

N

of fowls, some sweet potatoes (of these, however, one may eat only very sparingly), and some of the small oranges which grow there—sweet, indeed, and grateful.

Here I first learnt how useful a culinary aid the cocoa-nut is as an article of food, and how delicious the water it contains is as a beverage. It is almost impossible for you to understand what a boon it was to us in Timor-laut. When recovering from a fever attack, my greatest comfort was the water from the young cocoa-nut; and when this is extracted, on breaking the nut a thin layer of delicious pulp, of the colour and consistency of thin corn-flour, can be scraped off. The hard part of mature nuts is grated, and, when boiled, the oil skimmed off is used for frying. When the oil is made daily, the flavour given to food cooked in it is, I think, delicious; but when it is the least rancid, it is just as disagreeable.

It is, no doubt, troublesome to make the oil so frequently, for the grating is tedious, and it must be slowly boiled; still, Kobez was not so oppressed by many duties that he could not find time to make it himself. We learnt, at the close of our stay, that almost daily he went to the post-holder's house, and, with his *nonya's* compliments, demanded a bottle of oil!

Unfortunately our friendly relations had been slightly ruffled, and all through a goose. They had wisely brought birds of this family from Amboina, and, since their stay in the place might be long, they were anxious to rear goslings. Their house was built quite on the ground, native houses were built six feet from it, while ours was raised from one to three feet, according to the irregularities of the ground beneath. Under our house was the most comfortable place, without doubt, for the poor goose to nest in, and she chose a spot exactly under my bed. To my sorrow I was too often in bed, and was separated from her only by a flooring of split bamboo, which very much resembles the lath of a house in process of building. The other geese came about, and there was really seldom quiet from their cackling. In the night I used to wake up, sure that some one was moving in the apartment, until I remembered that it was only the goose rustling on her nest; and when I was lying in greatest prostration, after the delirium of fever had abated, in acute physical agony from rheumatic pain in every part of the body, and with every nerve on the stretch, the shrill *skrāik, skrāik, skrāik* of these birds used to cause me to jump quite out of bed from the start and sudden fright. I bore

it as best I could, though I felt sometimes as
if it would make me mad, for I could understand what a disappointment it would be to the
post-holder's wife to disturb the fowl when it
had set. What a resource both the prospective
fowls and their eggs would be in such a destitute
place; besides, I really liked to see them going
about — they were the only immigrants that
seemed to thrive. H., however, was much engaged with calculations from observations with
his sextant, and measurements on the shore, and
when thinking deeply, the disturbance of these
creatures was more than he could bear. Frequent polite messages to remove them were un-
heeded; at last we sent to say they must be
shot if they were not taken away. Our neighbours removed them, and owed us a grudge ever
after. I can laugh now over the matter, it seems
too silly almost to write about; but you can only
faintly imagine what we suffered from this cause.

The men went in company with the post-
holder and the four men of his party, so that our
strength for defence, should an attack be made,
was very slight. There was Kobez, to be sure,
our clever cook and caterer, who would doubtless
show himself as ready in fighting as in his right-
ful sphere!

Towards sundown one day, while they were still absent, H. was getting up from a very bad attack of fever. Rolled in all the clothes he had, he had just sunk into his chair, when a terrific shot startled us and the whole community. Shouts of "Kaleobar!" resounded everywhere, and the villagers, every man with his arrows and javelins ready, ran swiftly to the barricades in wild excitement. It was like nothing but a disturbed ants' nest. The post-holder's wife came to our window and cried, "Master! master! come!" but master was already disburdened of his heavy clothing, and busy with rapid arrangements for defence. I called Kobez, but afterwards it was remarked that no one caught a glimpse of him during the alarm. I think he must have burrowed in the sand or climbed a tree. H. very highly praises my self-command on this occasion, but I am bound to confess that the latter resource would have been mine could I have scaled these smooth-stemmed trees, and could I have had the heart to leave H., so weak that he could scarcely stand. After one moment the feeling of fear passes, and the excitement of the emergency lifts one above any thought of self.

It was only a scare from the accidental discharge of a late-returning villager's gun: they charge them always to the muzzle. The chief's son came to tell us, evidently disappointed that he had had no chance to fight; but we were thankful it was nothing more, while we were so ill-prepared to meet an attack. This incident showed how tense was the expectancy under which our village was living.

# CHAPTER XV.

TIMOR-LAUT is a Malay appellation, probably given by Macassar traders, who come thus far in their curious prahus to exchange their wares for tortoise-shell and tripang, and is a name quite unknown to the natives. They speak of themselves as Tenimber people. It was long thought that the two large islands, now found to be separated by a strait, were one; but the natives must have known of two, for they speak of the northern island as Yamdena, and the southern as Selaru. Villages are dotted pretty thickly along the coast, except on the northern portion, where there appears to be no population. No black frizzly-headed savage people dwell in the interior, as has been supposed: there are no inhabitants there. The old Chinese gentleman in Amboina, who was so kind to us, blames the inhabitants of some of these islands for kidnapping his son. He sailed in command of one of his father's vessels, and in this neighbourhood the natives had attacked him and taken him captive. All attempts to find him had been fruitless : his father thinks that, when they saw a vessel approaching, they hurried him off some distance inland.

They do have slaves in some parts, but there were none in our village. One day a large prahu drew near, and was moored to the beach, not far from our dwelling. The company came on shore, and stayed, making merry with our villagers for two days : all that time, before my eyes, a Papuan woman was tied to the mast, with not more than a yard of rope. Everything necessary to cook for the company, fire and all, was within this limited range, where she toiled all day, no one speaking to her or heeding her. I had a burning desire to go and cut her free; but we should have been murdered for my pains : and where was the poor creature to go to? There was no food and no fresh water in the interior; and besides, they would have hunted her down at once.

There are no mountains in the group, excepting a cone, rising about 2000 feet, in the west-

ern part. There are no fresh - water streams.
The island is of coral formation; and precipitous cliffs, 20, 30, 60, 80, and in one part even
100 feet in height, rise nearly all round the
coast. Some of these are of very beautiful and
grotesque shapes—huge boulders, perfect arches,
dark caves, and fairy grottoes succeeding each
other in ever-varying form.

The vegetation grows on the scantiest possible
soil. There are some very tall trees, though
sparse, and in parts the low shrubbery under-
forest is almost impenetrable. Bright-coloured
flowers are not abundant; but a beautiful orchid,
of a deep lilac colour, grows profusely in the
coral crevices, often within the splash of the
waves. In spite of the men's dread of going
into the forest, the herbarium grew. H. often
went off from sunrise till sundown to the mainland and the neighbouring islands, and returned
with a laden boat. Only a miserable few of these
plants ever left Ritabel: almost all were consumed in an unfortunate fire—a heartbreaking
episode to both of us. Writing in my journal,
September 9, I say : " This forenoon, when quite
alone, H. and the hunters having gone to the
opposite shore for the day, and Kobez to the
well, a mile off, while I was sitting in that miser-

able restless condition which succeeds a fever
attack, a longing seized me to look out of the
door, for I had for many days been unable to
leave my sleeping apartment.  Fortunate im-
pulse!  Kobez had piled half-a-dozen great logs
on the fire of the drying-house (an erection, like
our dwelling and all the Tenimber tenements,
of bamboos and *atap* thatch, now, at the close
of the dry season, very inflammable), and left
them to the whims of a strong breeze, which, at
the moment I looked, had just fanned the fire
into fierce flames.  I sped into the village for
help, but met the post-holder with his men running towards me, attracted by the rushing noise
of the conflagration.  Without a moment's delay,
some of them cut great palm-branches to inter-
pose between the burning house and the overhanging eaves of our dwelling; others tore apart
the framework, scattered the bundles of plants,
and beat the flames with green branches; while
the Tenimber natives poured on water, which
they carried in gourds and bamboos from the
sea close by.  With what breathless anxiety I
watched the effect of each gust of wind! for the
thatch of our house—in which were stored several
tins of petroleum and spirits of wine, and a quantity of gunpowder—was already scorched.  Had

it caught, nothing could have saved the whole village from destruction, nor us from the vengeance of the people. At last the flames were got under, and I had time to realise that the few charred and sodden bundles before me were all that remained of more than 500 of the first-gathered specimens of the flora of Tenimber, collected at such risk and pains. I could not bear to stand on the shore, as usual, to welcome the home-coming boat; but long ere it touched, the ruined drying-house had told them the disheartening news of the disaster that had happened."

The Tenimber islanders recognise a supreme existence, whom they name *Duadilah*, and of whom there is an image in every house, on a bracket facing the entrance, with a platter beside, on which food and drink are placed every time they eat in its presence. In their wallets the men carry little gods, to which they talk, confiding all their affairs and bespeaking favourable fortune; and every time they drink they dip the finger and thumb in the liquid, and flick a drop or two upwards, with a few words of invocation.

They believe in an after-life, saying they go to a certain distant island when they die. This island is regarded with reverent fear, and no one would approach it when sailing in that direction. We bought a fish once from an old man who had just caught it; before he delivered it he asked us to wait a little, when he cut off the fins and threw them again into the sea, saying these would float the fish's soul to spirit-land.

They believe, too, in an avenging spirit. We were standing looking out one day, when we noticed a boat being urgently propelled across the bay. On touching, the single rower sprang out, and went straight to the village shed, carrying with him a small red flag attached to a slender pole, which he affixed to the house. Then, raising his head, in a loud voice he uttered what seemed to be a prayer, his gestures, attitude, and tone being those of one under the influence of intense feeling. When he had done, looking neither to right nor left, waiting to speak to no one, he jumped into his boat and withdrew as hastily as he had come. This incident made a deep impression on us. I have never seen any man more in earnest than this savage, and we were much interested in learning afterwards that he was cursing the village, because he suspected some of the inhabitants of having stolen his loin-cloth.

They do have burial rites, but these are not

always carefully observed. Those who die in war, or by a violent death, are buried; those who die at home are placed on the detached boulders of coral which dot the coast, or on a platform erected on the sandy shore. A chief, or one to whom they would do honour, is always buried in this latter way. A decorated prahu-shaped coffin is specially made, and the body is enveloped in calico. On the top of the coffin-lid are erected tall flags, and figures of men playing gongs, shooting guns, and gesticulating wildly, to frighten away evil influences from the sleeper. When the post-holder's child died, they were most averse to its being buried, and the family had to keep a watch over its grave, upon which they dared make no outward mark until the people had forgotten that the child was buried there.

If a man loses his head in war, a cocoa-nut is placed in the grave to represent the missing member, and to deceive and satisfy his spirit. When a body is decomposed, one of the family brings home the skull, which is placed in a small platform in the house. But this custom is not always observed, and in walking by the shore one had to be careful not to stumble over the skulls which lay scattered there. One evening after dark a man came to our house with a great

show of secrecy.  On being allowed to come in,
he rolled on the floor from a sack half-a-dozen
skulls.  He was, however, a man of Waitidal
village, and perhaps did not feel any respect
for the dead of Ritabel.

Some of the bodies placed on the rocks are
encased in a disused prahu, sometimes only
within strips of the sago-palm.  These latter
soon give way, when the skeleton lies bare, and
is shortly knocked down on the shore by some
high wind or haunting bird.  A most sickening
odour used to come down the wind from the
north after rain, and at all times our men were
very unwilling to go past that quarter : they said
the smell gave them fever.  We sometimes went,
for very beautiful butterflies flitted about these
rocks, and, as I have said, the boulders are of the
most fantastic shapes.  Once we were lured on
some miles along the beach by curiosity to see
what freak of form would next present itself.

And now I have little more to tell of
this unusual experience.  The steamer, we
thought, was due on 20th September, but it
was eight days longer in coming than we
reckoned on.  The shot was done, the men
refused to go at all into the forest, the word
" Kaleobar " was in every one's mouth, the

attack was daily expected, and we had nothing
to do but long for the coming of the vessel.
From the 21st till the 26th I was prostrate from
fever, and I see some signs of impatience in my
record. Our men wanted to go back to Amboina
in a prahu trading for tortoise-shell which had
called at Ritabel, and which would take about a
month to reach Amboina; but H. was determined to keep them to help in defence should
we be attacked. H. employed himself in patient
efforts to photograph the natives and the vicinity;
but some of the chemicals were not in good condition, and the result was very unsatisfactory.
He tried to sketch them, but they were so
afraid when they saw what was being done, that
some burst into tears and others ran away. The
only way was to sketch them from the window,
while Lopez went out and engaged them in
conversation, trying to divert their attention
from that direction.

Early on the morning of the 28th, while I was
pondering whatever we should eat that day, a
cry arose, and Lopez ran in to say that the
steamer was coming—" he could not see it, but
the natives did." We had had one or two false
alarms, and I was afraid to believe the good
news. We hastily got the glass, and found it

was true. Far, far off, right in the light which was just rising over the horizon, was a tiny speck. Nearer and nearer it came, while we looked on with beating hearts and straining eyes till the long streak from the funnel assured us that it was really a steamer. Then the half-hour of high-strung expectancy till we felt sure that it was *our* steamer! Would she go east or west, or come into Wallace Channel? We tasted the agony of castaways in sight of passing aid. Yes! she was coming straight into our harbour; and, half-stupid from joy, we hurried hither and thither making final preparations, staying now and again to look out on the welcome Amboina till she dropped anchor a few yards from our door.

By 10 o'clock we had already sailed, standing where we had stood three months before, only passing from, not coming to, an experience which neither of us would willingly repeat, but which, nevertheless, neither would have foregone. Our sickness, privations, anxieties, and labours we felt not worthy of name beside the beautiful pictures both on the face of nature and in her creatures, the recollection of our pleasant relations with our savage friends, and the interest of our pursuits, which would henceforth furnish food for many a reverie.

# CHAPTER XVI.

*November.*

WE are now very much at home with Dr and
Mrs Machik in their pleasant abode, where they
have been already some time comfortably settled.
On arriving in Amboina, we found that the regular mail of the Moluccas was due in a day or
two. H. being anxious to despatch the most
important of his collections to Europe by this,
the first opportunity, we laboured incessantly at
labelling and packing, the task occupying the
greater part of the nights as well as the days
—a great strain while so weakened by fever.

We have now settled into a pleasant routine,
in which we continue the work in a more
leisurely way. The doctor being himself a keen

o

scientist, he and H. have as unfailing enjoyment
in each other's society as my sister-like friend,
his wife, and I have in our happy companion-
ship. Mrs Machik has a perfect mania for
tidiness, but she endures with the kindest for-
bearance the litter of our treasures scattered in
verandah and apartment. Although I have
some qualms on her account, I must also have
regard to H.'s oft-reiterated prayer "not to tidy
away his things." I have some lurking doubts
on the subject, but he ever assures me that
"there is method in his disorder." In a wander-
ing and hut life a great complacency gradually
comes over the most fastidious nature, and
happily blunts the edge of one's fidgetiness.
At first I fretted sorely over the thick dusting
of powder which constantly falls in a hut made
from green bamboos. This is the work of a tiny
insect, which commences to bore in the reed the
moment it begins to dry. Books, instruments,
and every level surface are covered in the morning, and when dusted, the gentle shower soon
coats all again. I now reason that nothing could
be cleaner than this fine sawdust, which can be
whisked away with a feather, or blown with a
breath, when anything is to be used.

The Machiks are Hungarian; they have been

nearly ten years in the East Indies now, and are
greatly enamoured of the pleasant life, preferring
the climate to that of Europe. Two girls who
inherit the mother's beauty, Irma and Ilka (the
Mary and Ellen of English), and a most precoci-
ous spirited boy of four, are growing up around
them. My converse with them is in German,
but H. and the doctor fall generally into the
ready Malay, which, with the aid of Latin,
serves them in the most learned discussions.
From these friends we have an excellent opportunity of gaining information on all subjects
connected with life in the archipelago, for they
have had experience of many parts of it while
stationed at the different garrisons.

Before I tell you of social life in Amboina, I
must turn for a few minutes to speak of our
voyage here from the Tenimber Islands, and
particularly to mention one person to whom we
owe much, the chief officer of the vessel, an ideal
sailor of the old type. We quite intrigued to
waylay him for a few minutes' talk when we
saw him approach with his steadying.gait, learnt
in many a wild storm. He possessed only a
limited knowledge of sailor-English, but could
recount his experience or tell a humorous tale
with a power which commanded the listener's

keenest interest, while through everything shone his gentlemanly spirit. Tom Bowling must have been just such a man : may it be long until he " goes aloft."

We were the only passengers, — rather a matter of congratulation on the whole, we were so worn out from anxiety and fever, and as ill fitted in garb as in humour to mingle with those fresh from civilisation.

At Skroe we purchased a small black parrot, which was an unfailing source of amusement on the voyage, and is now the pet of the children of our hosts. It must have been accustomed to fondling from its former owner (H. says it was nestling in the armpit of the savage from whom he purchased it), but where it got its taste for tea I cannot say. As soon as it saw the boy bring afternoon tea on deck, Kera-kera came hopping along from the furthest corner to share with us, and would imbibe a surprising quantity, well sweetened, and with abundance of milk. We call it Kera-kera from its frequent utterance of this sound, and here it answers readily to the name when the children call. H. cannot resist the temptation to buy animals, which prove a nuisance, since we have no home of our own. He brought a tree-kangaroo on board at Gessir, which is now playing such havoc in the doctor's pretty garden that we must put it in spirit.

At Banda we visited, as usual, Bin Saleh's shop, and were tempted to buy some half-dozen skins of the twelve-wired bird of paradise—a creature lovelier than I had imagined among the feathered tribe. During the night passage from Banda our boxes had been opened, and these, with a skin of the king-bird, extracted. This last we much regretted. While lying at Aru, Lopez went a day's journey to the haunt of this lovely bird, and delighted us by bringing back two specimens in perfect condition.

On the whole, however, we have not suffered much loss from theft, although constant petty pilfering goes on. In Tenimber a pair of stockings disappeared, a theft from which but small advantage could have been derived, for to wear them would have been to proclaim the thief's guilt. The loss we most mourned was a large knife which had been H.'s constant companion during his travels in the archipelago. It had been given him by his friend, Mr Ross, in the Keeling Islands, and had served him in all sorts of work, from hewing his way in a Sumatran forest to carving a fowl. The very

last of our knives for domestic use was stolen
on the day of leaving by one of the crowd,
who stuck it in his hip-cloth with such a
well-assumed air of unconcern, that we let
him off with it rather than affront him.

It is a great pleasure to be again in a
civilised dwelling, enjoying the society of
friends, and having proper food. Amboina has
a pleasant little social circle : besides the European officers and officials stationed here, not
a few have made choice of the island to retire
to, because of its salubrious climate, and the
comparative cheapness of living. There is
amusement without dissipation ; to the studi-
ous there is ample leisure for study, only
perhaps the tide of life is too stagnant for
natures disposed to lapse into the indolent
routine of tropical life.

We number amongst our friends Mr Justice
and Mrs Van Deventer, a young couple about
a year out from Holland, and full of patriot-
ism, though

> " par l'étude
> Citoyens de tous les lieux."

Enthusiastic over their own literature, to that
rich store they have added a familiar knowledge
of ours. It was a happy surprise to find our

classic authors in the original ranged on their bookshelves, and themselves conversant with them all, able to bring up in discussion the beautiful imaginations of George Eliot, and to quote the noblest examples of English poetry.

These friends never cease to mourn that they did not know us when we lived so uncomfortably in Amboina on our first arrival,—a regret which we heartily share. They occupy an ideal house at the rear of the doctor's, where we now spend many happy hours. They are accomplished musicians, and join heartily in the musical gatherings held one evening a-week by our host, a most gifted amateur, whose love of music disputes his passion for natural science. Weak as I am from fever, the long walks I enjoyed in Amboina some months ago are now quite impossible ; but it is very pleasant to sit in the verandah with my hostess and our common friend Mrs Van Deventer in the cool evening hour, or pace the sward in front of the house, listening to strains from the best masters in duet from the doctor's piano and Mr Van Deventer's 'cello. Dr Machik has himself instructed, with infinite pains, his elder daughter Irma, who inherits her father's talent in some measure, and, although only a child of twelve, can sing in her

sweet treble the whole of the soprano airs of
operas such as Mignon and Lucia di Lammer-
moor, as well as of the most famous oratorios.

It would be unthankful if I did not mention
to you the courteous attentions of Colonel
Dimini, commandant of the troops, who has
presented us with an interesting ethnographical
collection from the island of Ceram ; also the
friendly welcome always accorded us in the
homes of Major Van der Weide and the senior
judge.

Housekeeping in the Indies is, as a whole, ex-
pensive. Although market produce is cheaper
in Amboina than in large centres, tinned meat
and other kinds of preserved food are very dear,
since they have to be brought such a distance.
Fowls and eggs have a large place in domestic
cookery, and the abundant supply of choice fish
in the island aids housekeeping greatly. A
bullock is slaughtered every day for the use of
the troops, the officers and high officials being
first served ; but the animals are small, and the
flesh is not like the juicy beef-steaks of English
meat. Potatoes are very dear, but are in daily
use : they are brought from the highlands of
Java and Timor. Good vegetables of other sorts
are, however, generally procurable, and the

young Indian corn, so sweet and tender even
raw, is served in various forms, each more delicious than the other. Fruits, too, never fail, so
that, gastronomically, Amboina is not badly off.

Domestic life, too, is made very pleasant by
the employment of numerous servants, some six
or eight being thought necessary in an ordinary
household, and where there are children, there
are nurses besides. The expenses of housekeeping really neutralise any benefit from the
large salaries which officials enjoy, but it is
doubtless necessary to live comfortably in the
exhausting climate.

Washing forms a heavy item of household ex-
penditure. I blame Europeans themselves for
offering no resistance to the system of each
month's washing being retained in the huts of
the washmen until they call for that of the
next. An enormous quantity of articles is required; the accumulation for one month is in-
credible—for people are very luxurious in the
matter of fresh garments — and they suffer
great deterioration not only from the destructive
manner of washing, but from mildew contracted
through being carelessly left damp. But there
is a more provoking evil. One morning I saw
Mrs Machik's *baboo* crushing the articles counted

out. On my inquiring the reason, it was explained that the lending out of the linen of
European families to half-castes and natives for
great occasions is quite a trade. The linen cast
aside for washing is scarcely soiled, and if not
rendered unfit for wear by crushing, it will
surely be lent out for a few cents to some dark
youth, to gratify his vanity by appearing among
his comrades with a white shirt. A lady who
was invited to a native feast, to her surprise
found the table decked with one of her own
finest tablecloths.

By 6 A.M. most mornings we have a "reception" of infants, brought by their *baboos*, and
accompanied by the elder children of the family
—fair, sweet little things, with faces blanched
by the tropical climate almost to the whiteness
of their own frocks. It sometimes happens that
in the same family, when one parent has a little
colour, one child is blond-haired and as fair as a
lily, while its brother or sister has jet-black hair
and skin as swarthy as a full-blooded native's.

H. went to the island of Bourou within a few
days of our arrival here, leaving me behind, since
I was quite unfit to travel. Just before he left
we had the opportunity, through the kindness of
our hostess, of seeing a native wedding, and I

must give you some account of the curious and interesting scene.

The bride is the only child of a native rajah, while the bridegroom, an Amboinese native also, affecting European manners and dress, is a clerk in Government employ. Three different evenings we had to give up to witnessing this celebration. The first evening we ladies went in walking-dress to the house which was to be occupied by the young couple. We were received, according to their etiquette, by the bridegroom and his mother, and shown the numerous and elegant gifts which had been presented to the bride by friends and acquaintances. It seems this giving of elegant presents is in imitation of European practice, and many who can ill afford it determinedly vie with their neighbours. In the course of a few months all would be sold by the recipients to defray the expenses of the wedding. While we were there, a seemingly endless stream of natives of the humbler class poured in, to the accompaniment of a rude native band, bearing in trays upon their heads their own offerings of confectionery, fruit, and simple products, all neatly covered with snowy napkins. The bride we did not see, she being still busy with the preparations at her father's house, but we were shown the bridal chamber, which quite took us aback. Flowing lace curtains and clouds of coloured tarlatan spread half over this room of bamboo walls, while pure white flowers wreathed the mirrors and the many pretty ornaments, such as adorn a European lady's bedroom.

The ceremony took place at noon next day before the civil magistrate, and about seven o'clock we attended, in evening dress, the reception given by the bride and bridegroom in the house of the bride's father. They stood in front of an elegantly adorned sofa, on an elaborate mat, and shook hands with their visitors, who represented almost the entire population of Amboina. Europeans, natives, both high and low, along with the princes of an imperial house suffering banishment in Amboina, and Chinese of high rank, pressed forward to offer congratulations in the same grave manner in which they were received. The bride wore a rich white satin dress, made in the old Dutch style, with all the detail of gloves, fan, &c., while her breast and hair were covered with diamonds and other jewels in native setting. Her *coiffure* was extraordinary, and rather unbecoming, but her *tout ensemble* was very neat indeed, and one can imagine the pains and scheming used by her

maidens ere she got decked out in a costume in
which she would probably never in her life again
appear.

The scene was indeed a brilliant one. In it
mingled the rich brocades of wealthy Chinese;
the bright-coloured robes, with wonderful embroideries, and gay turbans of Arabs, whose flowing white skirts relieved a striking costume; the
gold and silver worked garments of princes and
wealthy natives, who glittered besides from head
to foot with jewels; the fresh toilets of Europeans; the uniforms of officers; and the sombre
black of civilians. The walls were decorated with
shields and spears arranged in neat designs, and
flags and gay - coloured cloths depended from
every corner of vantage.

As on the previous evening at the other house,
we were, at frequent intervals, offered tea, coffee,
and all sort of spirituous refreshment, with delicate
confections and delicious cakes. The relatives
and particular friends are entertained on this
evening to a feast provided by the bride's father.

On the third evening our party was again
wending to the same house, where we were to
see a special feature of native weddings — the
bride dancing for money. There she was, looking much more at home in *sarong* and *kabia* than

in her satin dress, working her way up a long line as in a country dance. When she has danced some time with her partner, he advances, and neatly throws his handkerchief round her neck. She dances on, as if unconscious; but shortly one of two maids in attendance draws it away. She undoes the knot in the corner, and hands the sum of money enclosed to a male attendant, who writes the amount on a slate, and passes the money to the second of the handmaidens. Meanwhile the bride dances on with her *vis-à-vis*, and the handkerchief having been replaced on her shoulders, she draws it off, and gracefully casts it over her partner's neck, drawing him towards her with it to receive her kiss of thanks. The amount of the gift has been called out by the male attendant on writing it down, and the dancers adjudge the number of kisses that it is worth. When one partner has retired, the bride passes on to the next, to repeat the same performance. Later in the evening, when we looked into the ball-room before going, she still bravely kept her post, though seemingly tired to death. Through her efforts the expenses of the celebration of her wedding would be largely covered : we have since heard that she received over £100 that evening.

All the time she is dancing, the bridegroom continues a shuffling *pas seul* just behind her, holding in his hands wine and a glass, which he offers to each partner as he retires, without ceasing to move in time with the dancers. Coteries of natives of the humblest class, servants of the household and dependents of the bride's father, leap and bob around the skirts of the line of the "country dance," and sing improvised verses in laudation of the bride and bridegroom, or in reference to any noticeable person present, their sallies being received with shouts of applause. Europeans took little part in the dancing this evening, contenting themselves with looking on, since the occasion was really for the humbler class, who were later to partake of a special feast, already spread in an adjoining apartment.

The Amboinese are passionately fond of dancing, and are as graceful as they are expert in all European figures. The rich native women and many half-castes were present in their handsomest *sarongs* and daintiest *kabias*, with white stockings and gold-heeled "slops," and it quite fascinated us to watch how cleverly they could circle the room without once dropping the shoe, which grasps the foot only by the points of the toes. Any one trying this for the first time could not wheel once without standing shoeless.

A very free use of powder is affected by ladies of colour, which has a ludicrous effect on the dark complexion : it looked just as if they had been making pastry before leaving home, and had inadvertently let some of the flour get on their cheeks. Not a few adopt for such occasions European toilets, and they look very pretty indeed in pale blues and pinks.

One cannot help feeling that much of all this festivity is a mistake : the expenses incurred are far above the means of the parties responsible, and the effect on the Amboinese character is not beneficial. The value of time and money is depreciated in their eyes, and after a week of dissipation, and even rioting, they are less inclined than ever for work.

For some weeks there has been little else in the children's minds than the visit of Santa Claus on the evening of the 6th December. We all met to receive him in the club-house, a building in which there is ample room for such a crowded entertainment. Santa Claus came from the fort over the plain, in pretty much the same garb as Father Christmas, attended by a guard of soldiers in torchlight procession. He mounted

a platform, and after a solemn speech to the
awestruck children, in the course of which they
were again told what had been reiterated in
every household for months previously—that he
had no gifts for any but good little boys and
girls—he descended and mingled in the crowd.
To his particular question some little fellow with
the most earnest manner would declare that he
had been indeed a good boy during the year;
and tiny maidens would peep up from hiding
their faces in their mother's skirts to receive
their share of bon-bons from the great bag hung
round the neck of Santa Claus. The little folks
of Amboina must all be good, for before they
went home one and all received a pretty gift,—
secured to them, however, by tickets purchased
previously by kind relatives.

We do not hear so much in our country of
Saint Nicholas, or, to use the form initiated by
the Americans, Santa Claus. To my friends the
Van Deventers I owe the information I now
offer you, in the supposition that it may be as
new to you as to me. With all Teuton nations
the night of 6th December, the name-day of the
good Saint Nicholas, is the feast for children *par
excellence*. He was a bishop who lived in Asia
Minor in the fourth century, and who was famous

P

for his love of mankind, and particularly of children. By them his name is at once reverenced and feared, for from their earliest years they are impressed with the idea that he is cognisant of their conduct, and will award them accordingly on his yearly visit.

Some thirty years ago there was a disposition in Holland among certain parties, doubtless under ecclesiastical influence, to substitute Christmas-day as the children's feast; but the bulk of the population cling to the old tradition, and it is probable that for many years yet the kind saint will meet his little friends on the evening of 6th December.

On 13th December H. returned from Bourou. He had accomplished a journey into the interior, only three times attempted in two hundred years, with results which were satisfactory in many senses; but he had learnt unmistakably that further work in the Moluccas under the present Resident was vain. We bethought us of the invitation of the Governor of Portuguese Timor to visit the island under him, and decided to leave by the steamer in which H. had just come. Two busy days of packing, a sorrowful leave-taking from many friends, whom the strong afternoon heat did not deter from coming with us to the wharf to wave adieu, and we were steaming once more straight for Banda, happy recollections mingling with the sadness of farewell.

# CHAPTER XVII.

*26th December.*

I HAVE hitherto spoken only pleasant things of
Banda. I regret that I saw that, on this last
visit, which will ever intrude upon more agree-
able associations. As usual we lay two days at
Banda, and as usual paid a visit to Bin Saleh's
shop, to see what birds might have come by
trading prahus from New Guinea since our last
visit. It was the sunset hour, and in front of
a house in the street parallel with the shore, a
comely Chinese matron, seated behind a strong
grating, was serving a dark syrup to the most
emaciated, weary-looking human beings I have
ever seen. It was opium. What a miserable
infatuation!—and the wretched creatures could
not offer even poor Maggie Mucklebackit's ex-
tenuation, when, " deein' o' cauld," and suffering

want of fire, food, and clothing, as well as a
" sair heart," she found consolation in a " dram."

Four days after we were drawing into Dilly
harbour, in front of the bare rugged hills we
had last seen six months previously, and soon
moored so close to the wooden pier, extending
from the palace steps, that we could see our
friends looking out for us in the verandah.

The joy of our meeting was damped by the
too evident signs that they had one and all suffered greatly from the climate. The little Marie,
who used to prattle so prettily on the voyage
out, had not long survived the deadly influence,
and lay in the Santa Cruz. The boys were thin
and sickly, so different from the merry lads we
had last seen; and all wore a wretched pallor
which it scarcely needed the recital we listened
to, as we sat together, to explain.

But though deploring that we had joined
them to run the risk of malarial sickness, our
friends made us heartily welcome amongst them,
and apartments were at once arranged for us
under their hospitable roof. Weakened already
by almost continuous fever, I dreaded unspeak-
ably the further suffering which the condition of
my companions showed me was not to be evaded.
With my urging to second his own desires, H.

lost no time in inquiring how soon we should be able to go inland to the highlands. His Excellency arranged an escort for the next morning, and along with his eldest son, who is Government secretary, H. set out to select a site for a hut on the hills. They brought back a glowing account of the exhilarating atmosphere and the magnificent view to be had from a height of 2000 feet, and a bouquet of sweetly scented roses gathered on the spot added confirmation to their descriptions of the charms of the place. It was some days until arrangements could be made and men collected to go to commence building. These we spent happily with our friends, resuming the pleasant intercourse of the ship, and with much to tell on either side of the time between, as we sat out on the wooden pier in the moonlight, with the water lapping soothingly on the steps.

The Palazzio is a long one-story building at the western extremity of the town, only about thirty yards back from the margin of the sea. Despite its rather neglected surroundings, it is a not altogether undesirable place in which to dwell, and there is ample accommodation for a large family party. The long dining-room runs behind a series of apartments which open into it as well as into the front verandah. The verandah extends the length of the building but for two projecting wings, which are the boudoirs of Madame and her daughter-in-law respectively. One beautiful apartment is seldom opened, the Hall of State, where at one end is a chair for the King or his representative on a velvet-floored dais under a rich silken canopy, above which a large painted portrait of his Majesty looks down.

The town of Dilly runs quite a mile along the shore, and has a rather imposing aspect on approaching from the sea, but a walk through its streets leaves a depressing effect on the spirits. It is not a lively place : no traveller will of choice visit Dilly, for its reputation as the unhealthiest port of the archipelago is not undeserved, and the report that one night passed in its miasmal atmosphere may result fatally deters any who would, except of necessity, go there. Those who are appointed here make up their minds, shortly after arrival, that they will go as soon as possible : what matters it that your house be pretty, or your garden a feast for the eyes? Fever-stricken people and places are recognisable at a glance ; the pale faces and enduring air of the residents explain the lifeless town and dilapidated buildings.

By streets lined with trees you pass on right
and left the hospital, the fort, the prison, the
pretty church, the Government offices, the custom-house, and here and there dwellings of the
Europeans and the wealthiest natives. On these
merge the shops of the prosperous Chinese and
Arab traders, whose adaptability to any climate
permits them fair health even in Dilly, and
round whose neat dwellings the graceful vine
thrives on arched trellises. Coteries of native
huts dot the environs, and there is a village for
the Indians from Goa, who have gradually found
their way here in the intercourse of this dependency of Portugal with its possession on the coast
of India; while another in an opposite direction
is specially for the improvident rollicking sons
of Africa, who, in service of their masters, or
perhaps in banishment, rear their descendants
and end their days far from the shores of their
native Mozambique.

The roads, except just within the town, are
unfit to be driven over, broken bridges and the
devastations of floods rendering this mode of
passage out of the question. The Timor ponies
are very fleet, but very naughty, and evidently
consider a carriage behind them an indignity to
be resented by the most intractable behaviour.

But there are sweet glades and gentle slopes
and bits of picturesque scenery within riding
distance, if you do not object to the roughness
of a dry river-bed, and pell-mell galloping in
pursuit of a native guide, who ignores your
prayer for a more leisurely progression, and
speeds ever ahead on his saddleless steed with
legs and arms flying out like the sails of a
windmill.

Timor is the least remunerative of all Portugal's dependencies, because its resources are not
developed, nor trade in its products encouraged,
and there seems no inclination to venture the
necessary outlay. No more enlightened direction could be desired than that of the urbane
and energetic Governor, our host: he has a
scheme to plant the swamp with cinchona, and
projects the removal of sundry hindrances to
Dilly's prosperity. But what can any one do
without funds?

Dinner here is at 4 P.M., perhaps rather a trying arrangement in the climate, for at 3.30,
when we go to dress, it is the hottest hour of the
day. At this hospitable board, where many
guests are welcomed, the meal is often prolonged
till nearly 6 o'clock; then the carriage is waiting,
and there is just time to drive rapidly through

the town and come trotting home by the sea-
coast road as the red sun dips behind the
horizon.

It is by no means unusual for three or four of
the family to be absent from table through sickness.

" Where is Henrique this morning ? "

" He stays in the verandah, madame ; a fever
attack is coming on."

" Is Mademoiselle I—— unable to come to
breakfast ? " we would inquire.

" She is still so weak from yesterday's fever
that she cannot join us."

A servant is sent to tell Senhor Fontes that
breakfast is now served.

" Senhor Fontes cannot come ; he has already
strong fever."

As we sit in the verandah in the forenoon
sewing or reading, one will suddenly utter a cry,
and rise from her chair. A glance at the
blanched face, blue lips, and bloodless fingers
explains the cause ; and if the attack is slight
the sufferer will rejoin us at dinner, feeble and
pale, to sip a little chicken-broth.

No one makes any fuss when another is prostrate—it is the exception to be free ; but sometimes attacks come with such severity that the

shadow of death hovers over the household. One morning Louis, the eldest of the boys, was talking with the others in high spirits, when he suddenly fell back. He lay for days unconscious, while every possible remedy by blistering and otherwise was tried; but it was many weeks ere he was able to move, partly from the serious nature of his attack, and perhaps as much from the severe wounds caused in the efforts to restore him, such wounds being most obstinate in healing in this climate.

The church, monastery, and convent of Dilly are the only buildings in faultless repair. One must know the people and climate fully to comprehend the patience and endurance that have been called forth to effect the civilising influence which undoubtedly rewards their efforts.

The altars and internal decorations of the church are exceedingly pretty; and but that the drive to morning mass was through scents and sounds which bear to the senses that meed of sweetness peculiar to the tropics—but that the lace-trimmed surplices of the lads who wait at the altar are incongruous with the bright-coloured *sarongs*, which do not cover their bare black feet—but that it is a dusky native that creeps up the aisle to confessional,—one might

forget the fact of being so very far from the
cradle of Roman Catholicism and the currents
of civilisation.

To think that these sweet-voiced choristers,
who, till they became students at the monastery
school, lived in savage freedom in the wild
mountains in the interior, chant the Latin
liturgy thus unfalteringly !

Nothing could be more picturesque than the
scene on feast-days.   To the right of the aisle
the ladies of our party in graceful mantilla; to
the left, officers in epaulette and decoration mingling with the few European residents of Dilly in
sombre black; the band of the troops standing
between in gay uniform, with their glistening instruments ready to be upraised at the elevation of
the Host; farther back, in a pewless space, native
dames in smothering veils and ten-width black
silk gowns, who balloon their skirts on gaudy mats
spread by gaily dressed attendants, who squat
on the corners to fan their lady; behind these
humble native women, seated on the bare flags,
nursing their infants and keeping their little
ones orderly; near the open door, stretching his
neck that he may lose none of the spectacle,
towers a beaming-faced negro, in pure white
jacket; leaning on the pillars of the porch is a

native rajah from the interior, in all his savage
splendour, come to look on the forms of the faith
he has ostensibly embraced but cannot mentally
grasp; and out in the sunshine, under shadowy
hibiscus trees, a medley crowd of all the nationalities Dilly can boast.

On Christmas Eve we attended midnight
mass to celebrate the birth at Bethlehem, and
viewed a somewhat similar scene under the weird
charm of brilliant moonlight. That I may not
weary you with description, I shall only momen-
tarily hold before you one or two vignettes,
which remain more clearly impressed on my
mind than others. The priests in gorgeous robes
moving to and fro before the illuminated altars;
the mass of human beings crowding the grey
stone building out to the door, where they were
better individualised by the inshining moon-
beams than by the sparsely scattered lamps;
intervals when we retired from our place in the
nuns' gallery, away from light and sound to the
cool gardens surrounding the edifice, where in
the fresh night wind the palms gently nodded
their plumes, and the broad - leaved bananas
seemed ethereal in the fairy light; and that, to
me, strange and striking moment, when at midnight a small image of the Infant was lifted from

its tiny mosquito-curtained bed, and held up to be kissed by all who would.

The monastery is by a long way the most inviting residence in the place. It is away back behind the swamp plain, and about 500 feet above sea - level, at the foot of the abrupt range of the Tiring Rocks. The priests are greatly beloved by the people, and are indefatigable in their work amongst them. In a morning walk you are sure to meet several of them cantering along on their small ponies, with the long black skirts of their coats floating behind them, as they go to visit the sick and the dying, or hasten to some tiny outlying edifice for the benefit of those who will not come to the imposing church in the town. Lahany is a picturesque spot by a foaming stream. The priests' neat domicile occupies the centre of a square of well - kept houses for the boys, vines flourish on the walls, and the garden is fruitful and gay. Over a hundred boys are being educated, and the result is most encouraging, some being such apt pupils and developing such qualities, that they go out as missionaries to other possessions of Portugal.

The site of the convent has not been so fortunately chosen : it is right down on the shore, in the very midst of the miasma, and the sisters as well as the children suffer much from fever. One pretty young sister has just died from it. One cannot help admiring their noble self-denial and courage in performing duty under such dispiriting influences. Their dress must cause them extreme discomfort. They wear the identical stuff robes imperative in a temperate climate, with the close hoods and heavy veils; and since their life is one of constant toil, cooking, washing, teaching in crowded rooms, it is difficult to understand how they are able to endure the strain. The building is so neat and well-ordered, and the large company of girls, from about fourteen to infants just walking, owe everything to their care. Some are very intractable, and long ever, like caged birds, for their homes far inland and their old free life. Some are indeed surprisingly clever. One child had just finished a beautiful piece of work, raised flowers in coloured silks on white satin, for a priest's robe; and some lace for the altar, as well as some exquisite embroideries for church use, were shown to us, all done by the children.

There is no school besides these; but the want is not greatly felt, for there are very few Europeans except officials, and because of the climate

these do not bring their families when ordered
to Dilly. The social advantages are therefore
very small, but the town can boast some remarkable personages. Madame amused us greatly
one evening by counting them off on the leaves
of her fan. "There is a man who was banished
here for stirring up insurrection; he with the
light coat, whom we passed when driving, murdered his wife; the middle one of those three
walking on the beach caused the death of sixteen
people; and there is another here who commit-
ted an extraordinary forgery. *Ici on rencontre
une société très distinguée.*" The penalty of
crimes which in the mother country merit
capital punishment, is frequently paid simply
in banishment to some distant dependency,
where the perpetrators have at least the miti-
gation of freedom. But what a living death for
fiery spirits to wear out life in the exile of
Dilly! Such a fate seems the refinement of
torture.

# CHAPTER XVIII.

PORTUGUESE TIMOR—SERVANTS—JOURNEY TO THE HILLS—
UP THE TIRING ROCKS—OUR HUT—THE HOUSE-WARMING
—— EXPLORATIONS —— THE RAINY SEASON —— SCARCITY OF
FOOD —— GOMA, THE INTERPRETER—VISITORS —— COFFEE—
PETROLEUM STORES.

*2d January.*

IT is strange to hear no Malay in Timor. This
language is heard otherwise all over the civilised
archipelago ; but natives here must learn the
language of the possessors if they will have any
contact with them. Our friends have considerable difficulty in making their wants intelligible
to their servants. The circumstance affects us
too very directly. Our Amboina servants who
had been with us in Timor-laut said they would
willingly accompany us to any other island of
the archipelago except Timor, " where their
language was not spoken, and the natives were
so different." I fear we shall have difficulty in

Q

procuring servants; the few capable domestics
in the place have been brought from a distance,
and are too much valued to be parted with.  At
the Palazzio they have a good head-man for the
table, who is also baker; and a splendid cook,
a handsome African, who is also hairdresser and
barber.  The latter takes the whole management
of household catering, and drills the fresh relays
of untutored natives, who, as part of their
rajahs' tribute, must become menials in the
Governor's dwelling.  *Baboos* are not to be had,
and were it not for good old Jacinthe, Madame's
faithful Portuguese maid, the ladies and children
would be badly off.

We had to consider ourselves fortunate in
securing the service of two brothers, Indian
men of Goa,—Pirea the elder, as hunter, and
Anea, a delicate lad of eighteen, as domestic.
Neither had as yet been bound to service, and
we are doubtful how they will bear the restraint;
so our chances of comfort are not great.

One of the two came down every day bearing
messages and bouquets of roses from the absentee
on the hills, and taking back the food which was
kindly prepared at the Palazzio.  On the fifth
day came word to me to be ready to start on
the morrow; the house was not yet finished,

but at my urgent request H. consented to let me join him, now that the roof was partly on. He joined us at breakfast next day, and early in the afternoon, while the sun was still very powerful, we set off for Fatunaba. Follow us riding through the tree-shaded streets, out over the great stretch of green plain that offers no manner of protection from the fierce rays of the sun, to the grateful shade of the tall cocoa-nut and broad-leaved banana trees amid which clusters the African village; and on between odorous hedges to a lovely bit of verdure, where gay butterflies flit among scenting shrubs, and birds flutter high above among lofty branches.

Then down the bank of a river-bed to pick our way among boulders and other obstacles, a scramble up the opposite bank, and we were traversing a mile of sandy, rocky soil, which, baked in the long day's sun, reflected its heat with sickening strength, while the slanting rays themselves fell full on our backs. Before us to the right, on the other side of a gorge, was the last outpost of civilisation—the monastery school of Lahany, and passing this we were at the base of the steep spurs called Fatunaba, or Tiring Rocks.

Some sparse shade there was as we wound round the face of a precipitous cliff; and when

we had emerged from the bed of a torrent, where
the ponies slid in the slime and slipped on the
smooth stones, the day had somewhat declined
—a needed relief, for real effort now awaited us.
Without daring a pause, lest the animals should
lose the forward impetus as they panted upwards, leaping and clambering, with only an
occasional straggling tree-root or a jutting rock
to afford foothold, for half an hour we mounted
that torrent-washed steep, keeping our seats
only by a firm grasp on the mane, and longing
for the level.  It came at length, a smooth and
green plateau, which after a few hundred yards
narrowed into a path by the flank of a deep
glen, so broken that a slip over the precipice
seemed inevitable.  But we passed that danger,
and mounted out of another gorge to face the
sharpest ascent we had encountered.  H. dis-
mounted and kept by my bridle, encouraging
me with the assurance that this was the last
really hard part of the way.  With a grateful
feeling towards the good little steeds, which
seemed as much at home on such steeps as a
chamois in its wild native haunts, we finally
ascended a gradual slope, with time to look
around on the repetition on either hand of spur
and valley and village cluster reposing in the

soft evening light, and back to the distant town,
bathed in crimson hues from the setting sun,
till we had again to give attention to the
path : first a water-course, with rocks bared
and polished by torrents, where the ponies had
to leap from ledge to ledge, and then a passage
through dense forest, where we had to be prepared to urge them over a fallen tree, or to
lift our legs over their necks as they pressed
between stems scarcely wide enough apart for
them to squeeze through.

"Why do people live in Dilly when it is so
sickly ? Why do they not make dwellings on
the hills ? " were questions I had often pro-
pounded to H. I have a satisfactory answer
now. It would be easier to plant the swamp
than to make a good road to the mountains.

When the gathering shadows made the way
dim, we turned aside from the spur we had been
climbing, brushing apart with uplifted arms the
tall grass which bent over the path from the wall-
like bank on the left, and soon came upon a
plateau nestling on the shoulder of the hill. Here
was my new abode, though it was too dark to
see more than its outline. After an inspection
by lamplight and a make-shift meal, I was ready
for my couch under the only roofed-in corner,

and retired with high hopes for the morrow.
Perhaps it was the keen air at this elevation
that enabled me to enjoy refreshing sleep in
spite of the protracted talking and unceasing
coughing of the large company of natives who
occupied the verandah, to be in readiness to continue housebuilding early next day.

The half had not been told! With the first
faint appearance of the dawn I was on the
verandah, waiting the withdrawal of the curtains of night. With the marvellous quickness
of the awakening tropical day, the brilliant
morning sun lit up the scene, and I looked
down the steep valley at my feet, away over
the forest and the green plain and the town,
out to the vast stretch of sea, set with the
prominent isle of Kambing, and enclosed by two
high promontories, the abruptness of whose
outline was broken by trending islets. H. led
me to the top of the steep ridge against which
our little homestead nestles, whence the view
is still wider; but I agree with him that the
outlook from our own verandah is the more
pleasing, the valley straight before us with
symmetrical enclosing ridges forming a shapely
picture. Then we turned downwards past the
rose-bush on the way to the stream, brushing

through a narrow path between luxuriantly healthy coffee-trees covered with forming fruit (I have just missed seeing the blossom, which is lovely against the burnished leaves), and coming out on a small cascade of clear cold water under a canopy of the tallest trees I have ever seen.

The slopes by the path to the stream are covered with pine-apples, which will be ripe in about a month. It seems this is a garden (mostly of nature's tending to all appearance) belonging to a well-to-do native in the town; and when the products are in season his servants come to gather them in, and lodge in a wretched hut which stands by the path. A creature more like a monkey than a human being — an old, shrivelled, and very small woman on closer inspection—sat under the sloping roof, devouring an unripe mango. She is, it seems, a sort of watcher, who lets the owner know when produce is ready for market, and lives here alone. So much for our next neighbour.

But there was still work to do; the house was far from finished. The one disagreeable element in all my delight was the presence of that wild intractable set of builders. The hut is really very unsatisfactory. The interpreter failed to come, and as the men do not understand a word

H. says, they scarcely lay a stick as he means it to go; so that in spite of all his efforts the house is very one-sided. It is on a slight slope; the floor touches the ground at the back, and the fore floor-posts of the verandah in front are raised over three feet. The half of the roof sloping back covers the three rooms, and the fore half the verandah. The arrangement is exceedingly handy; we really live in the verandah, only retiring into the more shady rooms when the sun is in its strength. I hope I do not mislead you by this language; the thing is only a miserable shanty, fit for the last days of a worn-out negro.

It was not till three days after I came that the house was habitably finished; then we dismissed the men, unable to bear their presence and the ceaseless babel any longer. By night and by day twenty-three uncouth mountain-men were with us. They worked by fits and starts; half were always sitting preparing mouthfuls of betel and siri, and to my unspeakable disgust, and in spite of every sign of displeasure on my part, they squirted the red juice over the whole walls and floor. It was always late at night before they ceased talking and wrangling, and some had the most dreadful bronchial coughs, which towards morning got worse and worse. How thankful we were to let the house go without necessary finishing—without even a door—to have it any way to ourselves. On the morning of the fourth day, when at 10 o'clock they had still done nothing, we told them they must go; the house was finished, we said. We paid them, and expected they would instantly depart. But no: afternoon found them still seated, chewing and squirting. We could not understand what they waited for, and they would not heed our signs to go; but about 5 P.M. a shout of joy, which greeted the appearance of a man descending the slope with a pig on his shoulders, explained all. We gathered that they would inaugurate our installation with a feast.

Oh dear! such guests for a house-warming! They commenced to cut up the animal on the verandah, and made fire to cook it at the steps; but the sight was so sickening that we gave unmistakable signs that the butchery must not be carried on before our eyes. We gave them a second present of gin, and though they still grumbled that we would not allow them to bring luck within our walls, we managed to make them go about fifty yards from the verandah to divide the spoil, and to disperse to their homes to gorge it.

Large bamboos such as are generally used in hut-building are not procurable here—at least the men brought only thin ones. The spars are very irregular—in bed I can see the sea and the ships in the bay; and we have no door, because the posts are so much off the straight that it will not hang, so we have contented ourselves with a curtain.

The first Sunday after our arrival we set off to explore the heights above our dwelling. Starting, this time on foot, as soon as it was light enough to pick our way, we mounted the very steep path to the same spur we climbed in coming — the only open way to the heights. The road is pretty much the same as I have described, only without such deep gorges. Every hundred yards revealed a wider stretch of coast-line and a greater expanse of sea. What encouragement to proceed! What reward for the pains! The dewy hill-slopes awake to deck themselves in the glistening mantle thrown by the urgent sun,—the joyous chorus of the feathered tribe fills the heavens,—tiny beauties, bright scarlet, glossy black, and quiet grey, delight the eye as they flit hither and thither,—a king-fisher, so royally blue, shoots athwart the slanting sunbeams, a gaudy parrot balances on a

swaying branch, and a pure white cockatoo with
bright yellow crest nestles into the shade of
some dark stem.

On we climbed, under tall trees, sparse but
frequent enough to afford shade without imped-
ing the view, sometimes brushing through grass
which cut our faces and drenched our garments, clambering over fallen trees, leaping
little chasms, and ever and anon resting to take
in the magnificent and ever - extending view.
Plateau succeeds plateau, carpeted with richest
verdure, from which we frightened herds of goats
and wild pigs as we seated ourselves on one of
the fallen trees to rest our limbs, that ached
from continuous climbing. But buoyant from
delight, and exhilarated by the freshness of the
mountain air, we pressed on till the ascent became less arduous : stretches of glade, with " tall
ancestral trees " that might have grown in the
parks of the "stately homes of England," tempted
us onward ; and then with one other slight effort
we gained the crest. Standing in an atmosphere
quite keen, the freshest I had breathed since
entering the tropics, we commanded a view on
each side which held us dumb with wonder.
Right before us lay the land of Timor, with its
curious natural features of sharp-pointed moun-

tain and sudden gorge, lit up by the bright
morning sun, which revealed, among the wilder-
ness of dark green forest, fields of pale green
maize surrounding clusters of huts, and, like
little specks, the large wallowing-ponds for buffaloes. To the right "the line of the sea-coast,
with all its varied curves, indentures, and em-
bayments, swept away from the sight in that
intricate yet graceful line which the eye loves
so well to pursue." Sir Walter Scott still further
accurately describes the Timor coast, though
speaking of that of Scotland—"It was no less
relieved in elevation than in outline, the beach
in some places being edged by steep rocks, and
in others rising smoothly from the sands in easy
and swelling slopes." On the other side lay the
view from our verandah, but here we had another
thousand feet of vantage.

Lest the sun should beset us ere we could
return, we had to hasten away, sorry indeed to
go, and commenced the descent, collecting at
different spots the plants and other treasures
H. had gathered as we climbed. Down we
hastened, through the glades, over the springy
grass of the plateau, on to the steep path.
Stumbling, slipping, catching with the hands at
jutting rocks, staying the feet on projecting

tree-roots, now tripping, again forced into a headlong run to end in an involuntary down-sitting,—at length, hot, tired, hungry, we reached our hut, where at this lower elevation the advancing day made its shelter grateful.

" We shall go every morning, shall we not? It was like going to service to ascend to Nature's Temple with the sound of Dilly church-bells in our ears." It was agreed that we should.

12th February.

Does the malaria rise even here, to Fatunaba? Or am I only paying the price of the days I spent with our friends at the Palazzio until this hut was ready? I do not know, but these many days I have been prostrate from repeated fever attacks, with a languor in the intervals which makes the lifting of a fin-ger or the raising of an eyelid a trouble. The constant doses of quinine make me so stupid that I cannot write without great effort. The rainy season is now fairly on us. To-day is the coldest, most blustering day I have ever ex-perienced in the tropics, and I can take pleasure in a plaid. Mosquitoes plague us terribly, but sometimes a gust dispels them for a little, to our extreme relief. I do not know what I should

have done without cajeput-oil. A lady gave
me a small bottle on the voyage to the Moluccas,
and that the application has saved me many an
ulcer I am quite certain. The mosquitoes do
not care to bite when the skin is covered with
this oil. Some people cannot use it, from
aversion to the strong odour. Fortunately it
does not affect me much, though I confess I
don't like it just under my nose. This cajeput
or cajuputi oil is extracted from the white
(*puti*) wood (*caju*) tree, so named by the Malays
from its white bark, resembling somewhat that
of a larch in colour. The oil is not at all greasy,
the colour is a transparent green, and a strong
mixture of peppermint and camphor might in-
dicate its smell. The faint odour which pervades
an apartment some time after it has been used
is to me most pleasant, like those subtle scents
you imagine when you read Eastern tales. But
I dare not again recommend it to any one.
Mdlle. Maria José at the Palazzio has suffered
greatly from distressing ulcers caused by mosquito bites, so I gave her some of my cajeput,
assuring her that it was a sure preventive of
attacks from the insects. By mistake in the
night she overturned the vial and spilled the
contents, from whose strong odour she spent

a sleepless night, with such nausea that one must not mention cajeput in her presence.

We have now been here over a month, and are as delighted as ever with the beautiful situation. But the house has an ominous lean, and has now more props to stay it than were contemplated in the original design. H. goes out first thing every morning to see how much it has slipped; what with the tempestuous weather we are having and earthquakes, I fear the whole tenement will topple down the slope one day.

We have put all the mats and a waterproof sheet over the bed, and as there is not another dry yard under the roof, it is the storing-place for all articles which would take harm—clothes, books, gunpowder, food, &c.; and when a torrent comes we have to run and hastily throw the things that are lying about into it. We then get our waterproofs and spread our umbrellas till the storm-cloud passes!

And we have great difficulty in getting food. H. sends orders in writing (as was arranged) to the shop of a Chinaman who speaks Malay; but he never understands rightly, and sends the strangest things, for which, when our man has toiled up the hill with them, we have no use. The only flesh readily procurable in Dilly is

pork. Our men, being Mohammedans, will not
yield to my suggestion to carry it up, even on
the point of a stick; and only very occasionally
does Pirea return with fowls, although sent
specially to purchase. We have resolved on an
expedition to the town to make better arrangements. Excellent bread is to be had there, but
we seldom have it fresh, for it is too far to send
often for it.

> " Here, I have said, at least I should possess
> The poet's treasure, silence, and indulge
> The dreams of fancy, tranquil and secure.
> Vain thought! the dweller in that still retreat
> Dearly obtains the refuge it affords.
> Its elevated site forbids . . .
> . . . . . . the baker's punctual call.
> If solitude make scant the means of life,
> Society for me! Thou seeming sweet,
> Be still a pleasing object in my view,
> My visit still, but never mine abode."

H. went down alone to purchase food stores,
and to-morrow we are to have an interpreter, so
now our troubles are surely over.

Goma, the interpreter, is a sad failure as such,
but he is a good, willing creature, and does our
bidding to the best of his ability. H. says my
conversations with him over domestic matters
make him nearly hysterical from laughing. I
speak Malay very badly, Goma a long way

worse. He can remain only one month, however, as he must then return to his own island with his father and brothers, who are here from Alor boat-building. In the intervals of the duties to which I must daily direct him, he stretches himself on the furthest corner of the verandah to snooze, or busies himself carving out combs from bamboo. But he jumps and runs with a smile to serve me when I call. He is enchanted with our cooking utensils, and has already indicated to me which of the pans he would like to take to Alor when he goes. He is also enamoured of my comb, which I now carefully hide. One evening I heard a vigorous brushing, and rushed round, sure he was taking a loan of some of our tooth-brushes, but found to my relief that he was using a small neatly tied bunch of pig's bristles to polish his really faultless teeth. He does not trouble himself much otherwise with efforts for personal cleanliness. I give him soap and send him to the stream to bathe, but he returns as greasy-looking as ever.

We have still the two Indians. The younger is a nice lad, but evidently cannot stand the cold nights of the hills, for he is always ailing. One night we thought he was dying : he lay for hours insensible, while H. tried every means for

R

his restoration. Goma on this occasion, with earnest entreaty, begged a ring from my finger, and having placed it in a glassful of water, he anointed the insensible lad, and taking out the ring laid it on his lips. He never doubted the power of his charm, and was quite happy when, after some time, the patient opened his eyes. He made no account of the medicinal restoratives we had given, and the fomentations and bags of heated salt we had applied. The elder Indian we must dismiss ; it seems, when he sets out ostensibly to shoot, he goes to Dilly to sell the shot, and when he comes back deeply intoxicated, his statement that " he has seen nothing " is quite credible. When he does bring a few birds they are riddled all over, and he comes back so late that it is impossible to skin them that night, and next day they are as a rule putrid.

We had visitors last Sunday. Monsieur Bento da França and his wife, guided by Senhor Albino, were here. Knowing our simple *ménage*, they had the forethought to bring forks and knives for themselves, and beautiful leaves fresh from the forest served for the plates we were short of. I sent our Indian to the market the previous day on hearing that they were coming, with injunctions to bring fowls or flesh of some kind, and not to fail me. Late at night he returned quite intoxicated, with a piece of pork on the point of a long stick, and throwing it down, tried to turn aside a reproof by impressing on us what risk of contamination he had incurred, and what sacrifice of the requirements of his religion he had made, in trying to do my bidding. The flesh had been bought early in the day, and had lain exposed to the sun's rays until the man thought fit to return, so it was already half stinking. But Madame brought some delicacies ready cooked, and, with what I could furnish, we had an excellent repast. The party had started before sunrise, and while I was yet busy with some simple preparations, a joyous cry reached me, "Bon jour, Madame!" Looking up, I saw my friend riding down the narrow path to our hut, preceding her cavaliers, on a pure white palfrey: with her hand raised to brush aside the long grass, she formed one of the prettiest pictures I have ever looked upon. She was better mounted than I had been when I rode up from the plain, and had accomplished the most trying part while the morning was still quite fresh; but it rained heavily in the afternoon, and they had to walk every step of the

way back owing to the slipperiness, so Madame
has had days of severe fever as a result of the
fatigue.

Coffee grows abundantly in the island, and
is of excellent quality. We are kept in supply
by our friends, whose lavish use of it we have
learned to copy. Ere the light has come, I am
calling to our boy to make fire and get water
boiling, and with the first streaks of day the
aroma of this delicious beverage spreads over the
verandah, where we enjoy it and watch the sun
rise. As it is often 10 A.M. ere we have breakfast, we eat biscuit and butter with it. My
thermometer is the butter; it is occasionally
quite stiff, and if I have not noticed H.'s reading from his thermometer, or guessed the temperature from the fresh atmosphere, I could tell
it from the butter-tin.

I must not fail to tell you what real benefit I
derive from having with me here a small petroleum stove. Any of the same form we do not
see in England, but they are in use in every
household in the Dutch Indies. A lady can thus
herself prepare any European delicacy she
wishes for,—an effort not to be attempted over
a hot fireplace. They are so neat as to be an
ornament to a side-table in the dining-hall, and

from the constant current of air which sweeps through every apartment in this climate, the smell from the petroleum is never perceived. I was fortunate enough to procure one in Amboina, and I do not know how we should have managed without it. Before we go out our morning walk, the fowl is placed on the stove to cook; it simmers gently while we are gone, and when we return the savoury stew is ready. Our servant has the potatoes or rice already cooked, and while we partake of this simple first course, the second, in the shape of a pancake, is browning beautifully on the even heat of the stove.

Mountain-men carrying potatoes to the market pass down the hill above our house; when we need a supply we hail them, and so have always plenty of this vegetable, of excellent quality too.

# CHAPTER XIX.

*6th March.*

WE went down to Dilly this week to meet the
mails, when I posted my last to you. We de-
bated long ere I could decide to go; but the
prospect of a day with our friends was so tempting, that I risked the fatigue. On our former
visit we arrived amongst them just as they
were gathering for breakfast—hot, draggled, and
dusty; and we felt so uncomfortable beside them,
so fresh and cool, that we resolved to have our
man carry fresh garments for us next time, and
to dress in the shade of the last cluster of trees.
I mention such a very trivial matter as this to
bring home to you the nature of the discomforts
attendant on such a life as mine. Mdlle. Isabel
tells me it was a girlish dream of hers to be

*femme d'explorateur* (the history of the discoveries of the Portuguese is very fascinating), but she now sees that the life is not all romance and perpetual picnicking.

We saw the guard-ship sailing out of the bay, and knew that his Excellency had left with his family for a few weeks' visit to Bancau, a small town about eighty miles round the coast, built upon a plateau over 2000 feet, almost sheer up from the shore, where they hope to recruit their health. Only Monsieur Bento and his wife remain here—and with the latter I had some sympathetic housewifely chat over our domestic difficulties. The capable servants are gone with the family, and Madame is at the mercy of a drunken African. On Saturday he received a sum for the week's housekeeping; he was invisible on Sunday, and on Monday morning all he had to show for the money was a terrible scar on his forehead. We expected to get some one to replace Goma, who must go to his own island this week; but there seems small chance for us, when there is no respectable servant to be found for the Governor's household. The chief object of our visit, however, was to urge that men might be sent to repair our roof and build the drying-house for the plants. With all its happi-

ness, it is a great disappointment to us that we
are still living our tranquil life in Fatunaba :
there is work to do, the wet season is beginning
to pass, and H. is anxious to get away into the
interior. He would like to leave me comfortably
housed ; and there is no use making botanical
collections without a drying-house.

Recently frequent shocks of earthquake have
occurred. I do not know that any great con-
vulsion has taken place in Timor in late years ;
but those we experience are sufficiently alarming,
since one never knows to what extent the shock
may devastate. Many of the buildings in Dilly
are out of repair, as the effect of earthquake. It
is not long since the hospital was shaken to its
foundations, and some of the poor invalids were
killed from *débris* or died from fright. Just after
we arrived in Timor there was a very slight
shock one night. H. warned me when he left
for Fatunaba to run out into the courtyard on
the least sensation of another, and to keep clear
of the buildings. One morning, just as light was
faintly dawning, I was awakened by an unearthly
noise and flash and glare.

"An earthquake !" I cried ; "all the houses
are tumbling !" and I sprang up and ran into
the back courtyard. Darkness and silence only

met me. I returned to my room in bewilderment, thinking I had been dreaming, when a repetition of the volleying and rattling commenced. This time I fled to the front, and was inquiring of some of the family whom I encountered, as frightened as I, what it could mean, when a hurrah from a crowd concealed behind the garden wall recalled to us that it was a salute of crackers and a display of fireworks to celebrate his Excellency's birthday.

But we had a shock in real earnest a few days later. We ladies were sitting talking in the verandah after dinner, when the gentlemen rushed out from the *salon*, and severally seizing one of us, hurried out to the beach. A sharp shock, with a noise like the roar of a train drawing into a station, so paralysed us that we could not have fled ourselves. The sensation of an earthquake is unforgettable : feel it once, and you never have any doubt what means that sickening rocking of the very earth beneath you, with the swaying of whatever the eye fixes on, and the clatter of everything movable.

Since the last words were written, we have had an amusing domestic experience. We have been entirely dependent for some days on our own efforts for household comfort. The good Goma had to go : his people could no longer wait. Evening after evening I found him adding a knot on a very dirty piece of string—his calendar— and he became very anxious as the end of the month approached. Just as he was going, a mountain-man from an adjoining valley came past, accompanied by his son, a boy of about twelve years. We thought the boy could at least make fire and bring water ; and his father, tempted by a liberal wage, agreed that he should serve us during the day, returning to his home every evening. This urchin gave us more amusement and more annoyance than I can well describe to you. We were so much occupied writing, that we rarely came out of the hut till evening. Doubtless the lad found the first day very long and tiresome, so on the morrow he brought over one or two companions. With their play and quarrelling it was impossible to write, and we forbade any " company " in future ; so he took to slipping away at his will, and some days turned up only in the afternoon. On being found fault with, he " resigned his situation." Anything more comical than this incident I have never enjoyed. Although I understood no word of his eloquent speech, his splendid dramatic action was a most accurate translation.

"Do you think that I, who roam these hills at will, and never in my life was at the beck and call of any human being, will be bound to such degrading thraldom for a few paltry coins! Give me what I have earned, and let me go."

So we were quite alone for over a week. H. has been writing an account of the journey through Bourou, accomplished before we came to Timor. We relieved each other, writing and dictating from the sketch-sheets alternately, and the humbler duties of fire-making and cooking were no unwelcome change to tired eyes and cramped fingers. On one of the evenings the weather was very tempestuous, and the fire which we made to cook dinner blew everywhere, to the imminent risk of the tenement, and the lamps were extinguished as fast as we lighted them. By patient effort we managed to half-cook some food, and having improvised a shelter in one of the corners with some mats, shawls, &c., we went to eat it. But just then the rain commenced, and poured through the roof, trickling down our backs, dripping heavy drops into our plates, and, worst of all, putting out the lamp.

The novel task soon lost its charm, and H. went down to try to get some assistance. He brought with him Anea, the delicate lad we had at first, for a few days, until Matross, the man we now have, should be released from prison. To discharge the debt for which he was incarcerated we had to advance several months' wages —a foolish step, as we have found, for we are entirely in his power, and he knows it ; but what else could we do ?

Men are here now building the drying-house and repairing our hut. They are a very different set from the last, and their workmanship and good conduct have considerably raised our estimate of the Timorese. They are men usually employed at the public works, and their foreman is a man of great ability and energy, so that after five days' work a neat erection stands a little way to the left of our house. The foreman says our house is irremediable without razing it to its foundations, and so we have only had it patched up a little until we decide if we shall stay much longer in Timor.

In this district there are more pretty *tiny* wild flowers than I have seen anywhere else. We go exploring into the neighbouring valleys in our morning walk, often getting lost, so that we are forced to trust ourselves to the guidance of some native, who leads us by a short cut over

streams with boulders I am almost unable to
cross; but who, however, helps us with our burdens of beautiful spoils, which, on coming home,
we spend half the morning arranging in drying-
paper. Numbers of fine orchids grow on the
slopes, and round the hut we have many already
in a thriving state.

I am serving my apprenticeship as a naturalist, and have made such progress that I can net
a bee without getting stung, and I now know
the proper way to grasp a beetle! Large and
beautiful butterflies flit among the high trees at
the stream, and many a half-hour we spend there
in the hope of capturing some, but they fly so
high that we are not often rewarded. A beetle
found by H. among the petals of a rose, a moth
spied by me in the dark eaves of the old woman's
hut, and netted with excited caution,—these and
suchlike are our pleasures, filling the days of
this simple life "far from the madding crowd."

With all its drawbacks, we have here enjoyment of the serenest kind. The wondrously
beautiful prospect before us never palls :

> "Scenes must be beautiful which, daily viewed,
> Please daily."

We are out on the verandah ere the outline of

the friendly Kambing Isle is yet visible, to watch the streams of light from the eastern horizon touch her with wakening hand. Soon the mists creep from her crannies and crown her crests, ere long to float away, leaving the sunlight to dance on her ridges, and nestle into her nooks. Early morning past, she is coquetting with the wooing clouds, now all gay and responsive, again sulking in sullen shade. Mid-day finds her reposing on the breast of the cobalt sea, colourless with brilliancy, as if pale from the strong heat. Thus she sleeps through the long afternoon, till she rouses to wear her richest blue and regal purple as she asserts her stately outline against the soft-tinted sunset sky; and at last, when the monarch of day concentrates all brightness on himself for his glorious adieu, she slowly retires from view, and withdraws into the gathering shades.

But as I have said, to live this Arcadian life was not the object of our visit to Timor, and we have made yet another pilgrimage to Dilly to try to hasten arrangements for H.'s journey into the interior. He fully hoped to have been gone long ere now; but they say there is now no use in setting off until the rains have passed, and promise that as soon as Lent is over horses and men will be sent for the journey.

It was Palm - Sunday when we visited the town, and we had the pleasure of witnessing the elaborate preparations for the celebration of this day — wonderfully complete, considering that means of decoration are not easily obtainable in such a remote island. Infinite pains had been expended in the erection of resting-places for the procession, and the effect was really beautiful when the tiny altars were illuminated at night. The whole arches of the doorways were lighted by innumerable little lamps, made from halves of orange skins with tapers stuck in them; and various designs in the form of crosses, stars, &c., shone out over the entrance way.

After we had viewed the procession from the windows of the Government offices, we bade our friends adieu, having resisted their entreaties to remain overnight, and started for a moonlight walk home to our hut. But after parting with them, we were tempted to mingle for yet half an hour among the crowd which hovered in the glare of the illuminations. I was so struck by the grace and picturesque appearance of a coterie of Indians, that I could scarcely be drawn away. The men have a striking natural dignity, and the women a grace all their own. Two sweet

pensive-eyed sisters, wives of one man, allowed
me to examine their beautiful silver ornaments
on neck, arms, and ears, when I took the opportunity to try to discover how they manage
to arrange a single piece of scarlet cloth so as
to form a complete garment, draping gracefully
from shoulder to ankles. Perhaps the rising
moon and the uncertain quivering light of the
illuminations gave them a charm they might
not sustain in the full light of day; but my impression is that they are the most graceful
women I have ever looked upon.

It was midnight when we started from the
town. The moon was well up, casting long
shadows into the gorges, and making every
bush seem a crouching figure. It was very
pleasant as we plodded on; the path was almost as clear as in daylight, and the cool night
wind came laden with the scent of wild thyme
and the sweet odour of milk, borne from some
hillside where a herd of buffaloes would be reposing.

How tired I was when we at last reached the
hut! We had been astir since 4 A.M. of the
previous morning, and it was now nearly 3 A.M.
I was fainting from fatigue, and could not wait
till water was boiled for tea. "Give me weak

brandy-and-water!" I cried, and H. hastened to fetch the flask from our medicinal store. Our servant in tidying the apartment had ranged all bottles of the same size in a row. H. grasped one containing a yellowish fluid, and poured me out a draught. "Drink it raw; I am afraid for you," he said. I swallowed it at one gulp: it tasted strange, but I was too tired to care. Presently H. forced another draught upon me. It was an antidote, for the first had been from a bottle containing spirits of wine and arsenic, which had formed the death-potion of our collection of beetles.

To his fatigue was now added a night of anxious vigil, and for me followed successive days of terrible retching and strong fever.

# CHAPTER XX.

*7th April.*

I HAVE been already one week alone. I write
daily in my journal that I am happy and contented, but I am only trying to deceive myself.
I feel the loneliness exceedingly, and did not
know to what test I was putting my endurance
when I insisted on staying at the hut. The
trial is entirely self-imposed. My friends at
the Palazzio hold a room always at my disposal,
and have begged me to pass the time of H.'s
absence with them. A lady in the town, wife
of the shipping agent, has gone to Macassar
with all her household for a month, and she
with great kindness pressed me to occupy her
house during her absence. But the atmosphere
of Dilly oppresses me, so that I readily forego
the comforts of the town, and face the loneliness

of the hills. When I get down into the plain I feel that I am inhaling poison; a leaden heaviness hinders any enjoyment of the otherwise welcome intercourse with my friends.

I mentioned to you an old ape-like woman who dwells in a hut by the stream. Quite a friendly relation became established with her some time after we settled here. She is very shy, and seems to have a reverential fear of H., but to me she confided her terror of thieves, from whose depredations she is kept in extreme poverty. She often goes away to friends in the mountains for days at a time, and it became a habit with her to leave her hatchet, her pot, her knife, with perhaps some heads of Indian corn in a cocoa-nut—the whole of her more precious possessions—in my store-room; and on her return she was permitted to take a smouldering piece of wood from our fire to kindle her own.

I have previously stated that women do not serve in Timor. I could only have one of my own sex by me, and it seemed to me that if this old creature would stay overnights, make fire, bring water, and take letters and orders to Dilly, the arrangement would suit better than any other under the circumstances. Before the cavalcade departed she was summoned into the

presence of the native officer, who is guide and
interpreter, in charge of the escort. He told her
of our proposal, and mentioned the wage she
would receive for her services. She was in-
credulous that such a sum would be given for
my trifling requirements, and at first replied by
a mocking laugh; but when she grasped the
fact that we were in earnest, she acceded
readily. It was impressed upon her that the
direst punishment would visit her if she were
not faithful, and with every appearance of sin-
cerity she undertook to abide by me.

She goes about her own business during the
day, and returns to me about sundown. Long
ere she comes I am eagerly looking for her.
Think of my loneliness, when such companion-
ship is welcome! I have had three days of
slight fever, with great languor, and have been
unable for much exertion. As I lie in my chair
through the long day, not a sound breaks the
stillness,—I start when the chair creaks. Lovely
birds often perch on the rail of the verandah,
perhaps regarding me with as much wonder as
I regard them with admiration.

I must not omit to tell you a striking incident
which occurred as the cavalcade was on the
point of departing. The road they took is that

leading over the mountains behind the hut.
The laden horses with their leaders and the
human carriers had climbed the steep bank
which flanks the house, and were winding along
the crest of the spur. The ponies for H. and
the guide stood ready; we bade the latter proceed, for I meant to accompany H. a little way
on foot. Turning to me with a courteous
gesture, and with earnest mien, the guide thus
addressed me — "Madam, have no fear; God
will stay with you. Let no anxiety distress
you; if harm comes to your husband, it must be
over my dead body, for I will protect him with
my life." Then, with a bow befitting a courtier,
he departed.

The number of horses was insufficient for the
baggage; but on reaching the next "kingdom"
—which the word "district" might better express—those from Montael will be returned, and
if horses are plentiful in Turskain, more will be
sent back for the remainder of the packages.
On arriving at the residence of the chief of each
kingdom, horses to the number of those arriving
must be supplied for the forward journey, while
those which have accompanied so far from the
adjoining kingdom return.

I had to-day news of how they are faring.

As I feared, the weather is very unfavourable. They have been most uncomfortably housed, too. The way is indeed laborious. Impracticable crags bar a straightforward course; they have to wind down precipitous mountain-sides to river-beds, and mount the next only to repeat the process,—a toilsome day's marching giving but a very unsatisfactory record of progress. H. says it would have been almost impossible for me to accompany him, so that perhaps, after all, this loneliness is the less trying alternative. How often have we regretted that I joined him only at the hardest part of his wanderings in the archipelago! How I could have enjoyed that elysian life on the Keeling Islands, with their fascinating interest, and with no fever or mosquitoes to intrude. How easy and pleasant his life in Java, with the rapid post-chaise travelling and the hearty hospitality of the distant stations. How delightful that journey by river in Sumatra, from the interior to Palembang, when he leisurely sailed for weeks together in his commodious, orchid-decked, floating house, mooring on the beautiful banks or at any interesting village at pleasure.

Matross, our swaggering, fine gentleman servant, is invaluable on the way. He is in great good-humour, because he is proceeding home-wards. In the course of their march they pass through the kingdom of Bibiçuçu, of the rajah of which it seems Matross is the son-in-law. Far from Dilly, where he was in the bondage of debt, and relieved from the petty servitude of domestic life at the hut, he puts on all his airs as a member of a royal house. He forages and "requisitions" as perhaps no other could have done, so that his impudence has been on the whole serviceable.

*13th April.*

My old woman is already proving rather dis-appointing. She is tiring of the restraint of staying by me, and last night did not come at all. I begin to suspect that she is not quite sane. She had a fit the other night. Groan-ing sounds awoke me, and I rose and looked into her apartment. She lay quite rigid, with foam upon her lips, and made no response to my efforts to rouse her. Next night about 3 A.M. I heard music—of a sort, and saw a dim light through the spars. She was playing on a Jew's-harp, by the light of a curious taper of her own construction.

Last evening's sunset was quite remarkable. The few clouds to be seen in the sky were

arranged in parallel strata, and discharges of
lightning kept passing from one to the other.
At 8 P.M. the clouds still caught a little linger-
ing light, probably zodiacal. In these tropical
lands Night is of jealous mood, and will abide
no lengthened parting between Earth and Day.
Ever at the appointed hour she comes with impatient step to spread her spangled mantle in
the heavens, hastily trailing her sombre skirts
over distant scene and near prospect; and Day
departs, often with plashing rain-drops for tears,
and low-moaning winds for sighs.

14th April.

I was in Dilly this week. Last mail brought
the news from my friends Mr and Mrs Van
Deventer that they mean to change residence
from Amboina to Samarang in Java, and that
the vessel by which they travel will probably
call at Dilly. I saw the mail steaming into the
bay when I came out on the verandah at dawn,
and in half an hour, with my packet of letters
for despatch, I set off for the town. I had never
gone alone before, and at a point where several
paths diverge unfortunately chose the wrong
one. I landed in an unfamiliar valley, from
which I could see no egress. There was nothing for it but to retrace my steps and make

a more careful selection. While I was panting upwards, bemoaning the loss of energy and dreading the walk across the plain, which I could not now reach until the sun was high, a native suddenly emerged from a side-path.

There are two encounters which I greatly dread,—one is a herd of buffaloes, the other a single native; and I have been forced to give up my morning walks on the hills in consequence. When the former are browsing on an open slope, I can make a long detour, and, clinging by branches and tufts of vegetation, skirt the farthest stragglers; but when I come suddenly upon them pressing along a narrow path, their horns clashing and clattering as they race and stamp and bellow, I don't know where to turn. If I creep down the slope on one side, or scramble up the height on the other, the chances are that they scatter, and some take the very way I am struggling over, in their mad gallop hither and thither. You must remember that I am only a small and very feminine woman, and no masculine female with top-boots and a fowling-piece.

But even less willingly would I meet a single native in a quiet wood. The Timor men are most unreliable. They are inveterate thieves, and not at all shy with their cupidity. Sometimes I would suddenly find myself face to face with one of these dusky gentlemen, who had been crouching behind a bush polishing his knife. He would come forward with a surprised air, and I can imagine his thought would be something like—"What a strange thing! I must go and examine it." He approaches me, strokes my cheek with his filthy hand, tugs my garments as he inspects their form, walks back a little to view my parasol, and all with as much regard for my feelings as if I were a statue in a park. "Oh, this is the white woman who lives in the hut on the slope; she does not look much. There must be things as strange as herself there. I hear that the white man is marching over the mountains with men and horses; I shall go down and have a look at her dwelling."

To continue about my journey to Dilly. The man I met was one of the uncanniest-looking mortals you could imagine. If one such were to peep round the door as you sit reading this letter, you would fairly die of fright. He had a fatuous leer, and an expression of hideous cunning which made my heart utterly fail. My knees gave way under me, and I was ready to burst into tears, when suddenly I remembered that bulls, and even mad people, may be quelled by the power of the eye. A locket which had escaped from under my dress as I jolted downwards seemed the special object of attraction. Every dozen steps he turned to examine it, then he would stroke me graciously, and I, recalling H.'s injunction never to show fear, reciprocated by gently patting his greasy back. But I kept a firm grasp of my parasol handle, and never relaxed my unflinching stare, while with most self-possessed manner and easy nods I indicated that he must precede me. There was little use in getting angry: he had a large knife against my parasol handle. The only way was to divert him until we reached the confines of civilised life. For two hours I drove that man before me; but when we came in sight of the monastery of Lahany I got imperious, and commanded him to leave me. Then I sat down and gave vent to my pent-up feelings, for I had passed through the severest trial of my courage yet required of me.

It was late when I reached the town, and, hot and nervous, I went into the agent's house to rest before proceeding to the Palazzio. Sitting there at refreshment, I heard my name spoken

in the verandah. Mr Van Deventer had come
on shore to seek me, and report to his wife if I
was near enough to be visited. The steamer
stayed only a few hours. These I spent with
them in a visit to the Da França family, and
when they were gone I turned to my letters.
My friends at the palace said I looked ill, and
must remain overnight. I was really unfit to
return, and yielded to their persuasions, on condition that I might set off ere they were up next
morning, for I daily expected the return of some
men from the interior, bringing plants to me, and
to bear the remainder of the goods to H. With
two trusty guides as protectors, I commenced
the ascent early next morning. The pony which
had been provided for me I sent back at Lahany,
for I really prefer walking to the perilous seat in
an unsafe saddle with an untrained pony.

The sun's slanting rays were distressingly
strong among the sparse trees of the heights,
and I was ready for the shelter of the hut ere I
turned to brush through the long grass of the
side-path leading to it. I was sustaining my
fainting steps by the thought of coming rest and
quiet, when a very babel of voices greeted my
ears, and through the branches I could get peeps
of what seemed a crowd of people. This turned

out to be twenty-four men and a dozen horses, and Matross himself stepped forward to hand me a letter. H., knowing my dislike of the noise of a number of natives in close proximity to the hut, had given them the instructions, repeated to me in writing, that the ponies were to be tied to graze on the hill-slopes, that one or two of the men were to stay to do my bidding, while the rest were to accompany Matross to the town to transact some exchange of products intrusted to them by their own rajah. They were charged to commence their return journey on the day of arrival, and Matross was required to bring from the town fresh supplies for my larder.

When quiet had succeeded to this bustle, I had time to peruse my letter, which gives a map of the route taken, with some description of the country and their experiences in traversing it. The natural scenery of the interior of Timor must answer to Shelley's lines :—

> " How hideously
> Its shapes are heaped around—rude, bare, and high,
> Ghastly and scarred and riven !—Is this the scene
> Where the old earthquake-dæmon taught her young
> Ruin ? Were these her toys ? "

H. is delighted, and is full of the interest of his work, if he could be but sure that all is well with me. That he may pursue his course with an easy mind, I have carefully hid from him the true state of matters. What would he say if he knew that a band of thieves made a raid on me the other night, and lifted everything that was readily portable? A large bundle of trading-cloth was taken entire, with the clothes I had worn in the day-time, my washing-basin, a ham which depended from the rafters of the verandah, and various trifling articles which I have no means of securing, as there is no door of any kind in the hut. I was awakened by a slight creaking of the floor under their stealthy tread, and involuntarily called out, but refrained from any fuss, on consideration that it was wiser to let the thieves take all than incite them to mur-der me in order to ensure my silence. But I am very uneasy, and grant you that it was foolhardy to encounter the risk of living thus alone, with-out reliable protection. Matross did not return from Dilly till the morning of the third day, and I had to endure two nights of twenty-three men snoring and grunting and harassing my strained nerves with their sepulchral bron-chial coughs. But I could readily forgive him, for this secured me comparative ease of mind during the night, although their presence in the

day, with their jabbering, laughing, and the
ceaseless occupation common to these untutored
peoples—the destruction of parasites in the
hair—distracted me while occupied in making
an abstract of the contents of the letters received by last mail to send to H. The task of
answering them rather burdens me now. My
nerves have got into a strained state, and a fever
attack is creeping over me. I had to succumb to
it yesterday, and hope to master it to-day, but
I fear it is not to be put off.

Have you any distinct idea what this fever is
of which I so often speak ? Before I suffered it
myself, I used to account these malarial attacks a
trifling matter ; and so they are, compared with
the critical fevers, such as typhoid or gastric,
which we dread at home. These assail with
severity ; but if they do not prove fatal, they
leave the patient to recover, and probably to enjoy
better health than before. But if one is suscep-
tible to malarial influence, the fever is never
done : it robs one of all vitality, it saps the life
away, you can never count on a day's immunity,
you never know the hour when it will prostrate
you. In some cases the patient passes from days
of languor and *malaise* into the sleep of death,
and in others succumbs to a sudden paroxysm.

Persons of different constitution suffer differently, and attacks vary in severity in the same sufferer. Sometimes there is merely a great languor, with loss of appetite. The slightest effort is a burden, life is a weariness, and the future looks overwhelmingly black. Then there are short and sharp attacks, for which one seems at the time little the worse. In the forenoon you are in a burning fever; by evening you can sit up; and you enjoy immunity for the next fortnight or three weeks. But alas for you when day after day for successive weeks finds you delirious, reduced to such a condition of feebleness that you feel an utter hopelessness of ever regaining strength for the duties of life!

Slight attacks are preceded generally by an unwonted physical energy and mental exhilaration. No task seems impossible, and the busy brain is full of schemes. To quote Mr H. H. Johnston's apt words : " This first stage of the fever is by no means disagreeable. One enjoys the same sensations as those produced by a sufficiency of good champagne. But all exertion is disagreeable ; one feels content to sit and compose chapters of novels in one's whirling brain, without attempting to commit the fleeting kaleidoscopic images to paper." I have often felt quite hurt that H. would not be my amanuensis on such occasions, refusing to commit my brilliant ideas to paper, and only giving a pitying smile when I confided to him that I was meditating a poem. I used to think him very commonplace when he ordered boiling water, and asked me if the tea-caddy was handy.

Sundry twinges in the region of the neck and shoulders might give warning of what must follow, but the flights of the imagination do not suffer one to think of things corporal. You sit mounting the ladder of fame with soaring spirit, deliberating which of your many projects you will give the first place to, when a sensation as if cold water were trickling down the spine arrests you. There is no mistaking this symptom. You may feel rebellious, you may weep for very chagrin; but get into bed, and heap every garment you possess upon you. The lips are blue, the fingers are benumbed already; the rending ague, the burning fever, the soaking sweat, the prostrating weakness, will follow as surely as the day the dawn.

There is something pathetic to myself in my hasty arrangements when an attack seizes me. I get my stove lit to make the hot weak tea which helps one through the ague. I lay every-

T

thing at hand which I shall need during the fever, and put dry garments within reach. The perspiration which follows is surprisingly profuse. It is no exaggeration to say that one lies as wet as if pails of water had been poured on the bed; towels placed round the neck to catch the streams from the head are soaked in a quarter of an hour as if they had been lifted from a wash-tub; and when one has been rolled on to a dry mattress and assisted into other garments, the feeling of comfort is as if one were being tended after having been saved from drowning. This is the only pleasant moment during the whole attack, and I miss the care which I have never lacked in a stage of weakness when, to say the least, it would be grateful. I miss, too, the spoonful of nourishing soup which relieves the sinking faintness that succeeds the weakening attack. One would rather want it than make the effort to prepare it one's self.

Severe attacks begin with violent retching and acute rheumatic pain, to which delirium invariably succeeds. In Timor-laut I lay within the sound of the lapping waves, and I used to imagine that I was standing on the shore watching my head float out over the sea. I was ever making distressing efforts to follow it and keep it in sight, but it got lost somehow, and I got lost myself, till, as if awaking from sleep, I became conscious of being in bed, with a feeling of mild surprise that my head was still on. Any other consciousness is of extreme weakness. But you imagine the patient will, at least, have rest in this state of prostrate quiet? No, no; this is but a respite before the real suffering begins. Every pore of the body becomes a needle-point, and million simultaneous prickings cause you actually to leap into the air. Every joint becomes a centre of acute agony, and each limb a vehicle for shooting pains, which in passing out from the fingers and toes seem to tear the nails off with them. I have often been surprised on looking to find my nails in their place, for I was positive that they were gone.

And the restlessness! Fifty, a hundred times in an hour you change your position. Vertical, horizontal, straight along, cornerways, sideways, the poor body tosses and turns, seeking a resting-place. At last a spot is found somewhat reposeful; sleep, nature's panacea, steals over the senses; the fever patient is recovering—till next time.

My old woman never comes near me now. When I have had a few days of rest, I shall go

down to Dilly to try to get some one to stay by
me. Matross got intoxicated, and failed to
bring the food stores I require. I sent everything I had on to H., since they are very poorly
supplied in the interior, and have only rice and
eggs for present use. My fowls are of no benefit
except for their eggs, as I cannot myself kill
them; but I have traced them to their nests
amongst the long grass, and have always a good
supply of eggs. My hunt has to be rather a
wary one, by reason of a discovery I have made
that snakes frequent the vicinity. One wriggled
through the spars of the kitchen wall lately, and
when beaten to death it was found to have
poison fangs.

These past few days I have been much occupied, and have had no time to fret; but I do
confess to feeling somewhat desolate at the sunset hour, which was always the pleasantest part of
the day. I light the lamp early, and busy myself
cooking my dinner; for if I were to sit down to
watch the fading glow, and turn round to stillness and darkness and no food, instead of the
spread table, and the lamplight, and the crackle
and blaze of the kitchen-fire, I should surely get
faint-hearted.

I am not altogether forsaken. I have occa-

sional visits from my hillside neighbours (who
are, I suspect, the thieves; for they could note
the position of things in the day-time, and
readily lift them at night). They ply me with
questions about master, inquiring when he is
coming back, to which I always make the same
reply : " Soon ; he has only gone over the hill.".
But they have found me out! Sometimes the
mountain-men choose my verandah as their resting-place for the night, instead of going to the
old woman's hut, as was their wont. But they
are always off by dawn, to be in Dilly early with
their loads of potatoes for the market. They are
quite harmless, and I have no fear of them ; but
they have an insufferable odour, and they are
undoubtedly fearsome - looking creatures. A
stranger group than that stretched in deep sleep
around me last night, as I, sleepless, whiled
away a part of the dreary time in studying them
both in attitude and physiognomy by the brilliant moonlight, it would be difficult to imagine.

# CHAPTER XXI.

*20th May.*

THERE is a long blank in my journal, of which
you probably need no explanation. You guess
that I succumbed to illness—a fever as much
nervous as malarial. Day after day for a fortnight, ere ten in the morning I was in high
fever, and until afternoon lay in delirium, unconscious of my surroundings. At first I was
able to change my clothing and turn my mattress, and in the early morning came some little
strength, with which I made preparations for the
day of helplessness. I placed within reach my
paraffin stove, with rice, salt, and water, and
hung on a rope garments ready to change.
Every morning I meant to go out amongst the
grass to bring in the eggs accumulating there;
but high winds, which made me dread a chill,

prevailed, and ere I could make up my mind to the effort of dressing, the fever was on me again.

I do not mean to harass your feelings by any detailed account of what I passed through, and will dismiss the subject in a few sentences. It touches me deeply to call that time of trial into review; but I did not actually suffer so badly as you would be led to suppose from the circumstance that I was so ill, with no human being to tend me. The worst time was when I came to myself after the delirium, about three in the afternoon, the hottest hour of the day, when the sun was pouring in on me through the spars, and I was unable to change my position, partly owing to weakness, partly because I had gradually drawn almost every article in the hut within my bed. The rats, which at first confined their revels to the darkness of night, got so bold in the unbroken stillness that even in the day-time they tried to gnaw through my bed-curtains, within which books and boots and food had to be secured. My pillows had got pressed into nothing for want of shaking up, and under them I managed to push the bag containing rice. Thus hampered, I lay under the beating rays with stifling palpitation, panting for breath, and in a confused excited state, which coolness and darkness and perhaps an encouraging voice would have soothed. But the slow hours at length wore by, and the evening shadows gathered. I got cold enough now in my wet garments, and became so faint and weak that I would gladly have died. With a vague sort of pity for myself, I could not withhold a few tears; but I soon fell into a state when beautiful visions which I vainly try to recall passed before my sight, while strains of grandest and sweetest music added soothing to the inexplicably pleasing images. Then I lost consciousness in snatches of fitful dozing, to awake long before the dawn. Now was the only mentally clear time of the twenty-four hours, and with the greatest effort I roused myself to light the stove and make some rice-water, the only food I had. What sustained me was the determination not to die. The thought of H.'s agony should he come in some day and find only what of me the rats had left, inspired me to struggle for life. I seemed to exist in a dual state: one side would have sought pity and sympathy, the other scorned and scouted and imperiously forbade any such weakness, or the luxury of giving in to it.

At last my stove got empty. I could not go to the store to refill it, but I reached out for the reading-lamp, and emptied its contents into the cooking-stove. I had one little companion, a chicken which I had bought from a passing mountain-lad. It did not grow, and would not mingle with the other fowls; accustomed to sleep in the armpit of its former owner, it felt the cold of its unsheltered roost in the verandah, and with a fretful crooning it would come fluttering to perch on my bed. How it escaped the rats so long I cannot tell; they caught birds as large on the trees, and raced with them over the floor in broad daylight, dragging them hither and thither as they tore them in pieces. Any one who has never before killed a fowl must find the act very repulsive: in the state of my nerves it seemed little short of murder to slay the trusting little thing, whose nearness to me I had found companionable. I somehow twisted its neck, when I threw it from me as far as I was able; then I lay down for some hours in utter misery. At last I got up to seek for it, and made from it the soup which I believe saved me till aid came.

The third week the fever abated somewhat; I was more weak and helpless than feverish, although there was a recurrence every morning. I wrote a note for my friends, telling how it was

faring with me.  I meant to rise and try to walk
to Dilly; if I failed, surely some one would be
on the main path, and be persuaded to carry on
the letter.  By good fortune a lad from a neighbouring valley, whose open intelligent countenance had attracted us before, came past that
afternoon.  I explained to him that I wished a
letter carried to the town, and would reward
him well.  "No; he would not go among the
white people; he was a hill-man, and was shy."
I tempted him with coin after coin: he did not
know their value.  He consented, he refused, he
wavered; he little knew that he held me on the
rack—that I was almost stifled with eagerness—
I was really bargaining for my life.  At last he
gave in so far: he would go to the town and
drop the letter in the street, but he would not
go to the Palazzio.  Off he ran, and I lay back
thankful and exhausted.  But in three minutes
he was back again; rain had commenced to fall,
and with a native's dread of a wetting, he would
not face it.  My parasol lay in a corner.  I
pointed to it; he seized it and ran off—the fun-
niest figure you ever saw, with his red loin-cloth
and my blue-spotted parasol for sole attire !

About 5 P.M. to my surprise I saw him returning.  Close in his wake followed two men; these

he had met half-way, bearing a letter of inquiry why I had not written or come down. They took my letter, and early next day I was surprised by the sight of three horsemen descending the path. The doctor, with two European gentlemen, had come to ascertain the state of matters. They were quite shocked to see my condition, and two of them returned at once for a couch to carry me down, while the doctor remained with me. We had thought of the hammocks, but the rats had gnawed them in shreds. It was five o'clock when the chair and carriers arrived. Night would be upon us, and I begged to be allowed to remain; the food and wine I had had would have strengthened me on the morrow. But the doctor was inexorable. He could not return so far; I must go down to have nursing and restoratives. So we started. The chair was of no use. The path on the edge of precipitous slopes did not admit of two men abreast with the chair between, and I was twice rolled off. Ere we were well started night came down, and then the carriers refused to bear me. There was nothing now for it but to walk. For five hours we struggled down the Tiring Rock, with only the stars to light us. We had to grope our way, and on the steepest parts to sit down and let ourselves slide. I several times gave in, and begged to be left, but the good doctor encouraged me with infinite patience. At last we reached the plain, where I could be carried comfortably, and he rode on to tell our friends that I should soon arrive.

They at once sent word to H., who got the news of my sickness in mid-Timor. He never left the saddle for three days and three nights, and landed amongst us one Sunday morning, the sorriest sight imaginable—burnt and travel-stained to a ludicrous degree. I was then convalescent, thanks to the great kindness of Madame da França and her family, and we lost no time in returning to the hut, at which the collection of plants, &c., gathered on H.'s journey might any day arrive.

So we are again enjoying the old tranquil life. But I have frequent attacks of fever, and we have decided to return to England by the first mail.

BUITENZORG.

I am now under the roof where I commenced these letters to you. We left Timor very hurriedly at last. We thought some weeks must pass before the mail we meant to leave by should arrive. One morning, on coming out on

the verandah, we saw a vessel standing into the
bay.  H. hurried down, and found that it was
an intermediate steamer, but that no other
would be in for some time; so with utmost
haste all that we wished to take with us was
bundled together and transported to the ship.
We left everything but clothes and collections.
There was no time to bestow our goods on any
one capable of appreciating them : they were
left to be appropriated by our uncouth neighbours, and no small share fell to the old
woman who had so basely deserted me in my
hour of need.

The Governor's family were again our companions on the return voyage.  A great sorrow
befell them at the last.  The day before their
departure, Henrique, a beautiful boy of ten
years, was buried.  He seemed the least likely
of any to succumb.  He had been ailing, as were
all the others ; but it was a sad shock when,
after a paroxysm of some thirty minutes' dura-
tion, he lay dead.  I have just heard from
Mademoiselle Isabel that the good old Jacinthe
died near Singapore, and was buried at sea.

We had a very roundabout voyage here.
Sailing directly, we could have reached Java
from Timor in five or six days.  No direct

route, however, is available, and we had to go up to Amboina, and round the north of Celebes. We were all too ill to enjoy the trip; quite half of us were generally down with fever, so that the captain used to call the poop the hospital. But there were no passengers except ourselves, the captain was most thoughtful for our comfort, and altogether we got through the discomforts of suffering illness on a tropical voyage with greater advantages than are generally available.

We had no time to advise our friends in Amboina that we should touch there in the course of our voyage. I happened to be free of fever the morning we arrived, and with great glee at the surprise I should give Mrs Machik, walked off to her house as soon as the vessel moored. All the front was shuttered, and the doors closed against the heat, as is usual after the early morning has passed. I walked through the saloon, opened a second door, and was in the large cool dining-hall ere she heard me. She just seized me and danced up and down the room for about three minutes, calling out, " Children ! come ! Frau Forbes has come back again ! " H. went to the ship for as many of the Da França family as were not prostrated by fever, and we spent together a most happy day.

Just outside of the bay of Amboina we were surprised by a small tidal wave, which, sailing as we were in the smoothest sea, alarmed us by the sudden upset. Tables, chairs, sofas, books, eau-de-Cologne bottles, fans, toys, glasses, children, and we grown people,—all joined in the irresistible rush to the side of the vessel. The cry of one of the children, who thought she was going overboard, afforded us great amusement after everything was righted—"Mamma! I do not wish to go!" I tried to seize hold on H. to steady myself, but only caught sight of him and little Madame and a sofa trending off in quite another course from that to which I was impelled. During many months of sailing I have never encountered any disturbance more serious than a rough sea. In this region storms rarely come in moderation; nothing short of a cyclone in which no ship can live relieves the elements.

We lay four days in Menado, at the northeastern extremity of the island of Celebes. The inhabitants are as widely different from those of the southern isles of the archipelago as are Swedes from Italians. Their complexion is yellowish, and the hair is quite straight. They are noticeably neat in dress, and all wear hats.

The pretty town had been wrecked by an inundation the previous week, and though refreshingly green overhead from abundant foliage, every garden was destroyed, every road was washed bare or into deep ruts, and the base of each house was discoloured and shabby-looking. People had been wading waist-deep in their dwellings, and far into the sea rode a forest of uptorn, down-washed trees. A little child was picked up near the shore riding on a sow's back, where it had kept its equilibrium by clinging to the ears.

At Surabaya we parted with much sorrow and regret from our true friends the Da França family. They return to Portugal by Singapore, while we wait the Queensland mail for England. I have no words to express what we owe to them. Elders and children, they compose the most lovable family imaginable, and we found them as courteous and kindly to the stranger as they were affectionate amongst themselves.

Now I have done. We sail on 9th July, and when the song of the reapers floods the fields, we shall touch our own island shores. The beautiful archipelago we are so soon to leave behind us will, I think, from the discomfort and even danger of travelling in such a tropical climate, never become to any extent a resort for tourist voyagers. It will be left for the few who must dwell in it at the call of duty, or who travel through it urged by enthusiasm. Neither stimulus buoyed me up; I have simply been the voluntary companion of an ardent lover of Nature, the reflex of whose happiness I could not avoid sharing. But as long as memory lasts, pictures of face and form, of sight and sound, of day and night, of land and sea, will rise at call or flit before my vision; the remembrance of my sufferings will grow dimmer under the softening hand of time; and I shall be able to say, what I now only faintly realise, that they are not worthy of mention beside the value of my experience as a Naturalist's companion in his roamings in Insulinde.

THE END.

Some other Oxford Paperbacks for readers interested in Central Asia,
China and South-East Asia, past and present

## CAMBODIA
GEORGE COEDÈS
Angkor

MALCOLM MacDONALD
Angkor and the Khmers*

## CENTRAL ASIA
ANDRÉ GUIBAUT
Tibetan Venture

PETER FLEMING
Bayonets to Lhasa

LADY MACARTNEY
An English Lady in Chinese
Turkestan

DIANA SHIPTON
The Antique Land

C. P. SKRINE AND
PAMELA NIGHTINGALE
Macartney at Kashgar*

ALBERT VON LE COQ
Buried Treasures of Chinese
Turkestan

AITCHEN K. WU
Turkistan Tumult

## CHINA
All About Shanghai: A Standard
Guide

HAROLD ACTON
Peonies and Ponies

VICKI BAUM
Shanghai '37

ERNEST BRAMAH
Kai Lung's Golden Hours*

ERNEST BRAMAH
The Wallet of Kai Lung*

ANN BRIDGE
The Ginger Griffin

CHANG HSIN-HAI
The Fabulous Concubine*

CARL CROW
Handbook for China

PETER FLEMING
The Siege at Peking

MARY HOOKER
Behind the Scenes in Peking

CORRINNE LAMB
The Chinese Festive Board

W. SOMERSET
MAUGHAM
On a Chinese Screen*

G. E. MORRISON
An Australian in China

PETER QUENNELL
Superficial Journey through
Tokyo and Peking

OSBERT SITWELL
Escape with Me! An Oriental
Sketch-book

J. A. TURNER
Kwang Tung or Five Years in
South China

## HONG KONG AND
## MACAU
AUSTIN COATES
City of Broken Promises

AUSTIN COATES
A Macao Narrative

AUSTIN COATES
Myself a Mandarin

AUSTIN COATES
The Road

The Hong Kong Guide 1893

## INDONESIA
S. TAKDIR
ALISJAHBANA
Indonesia: Social and Cultural
Revolution

DAVID ATTENBOROUGH
Zoo Quest for a Dragon*

VICKI BAUM
A Tale from Bali*

'BENGAL CIVILIAN'
Rambles in Java and the Straits
in 1852

MIGUEL COVARRUBIAS
Island of Bali*

BERYL DE ZOETE AND
WALTER SPIES
Dance and Drama in Bali

AUGUSTA DE WIT
Java: Facts and Fancies

JACQUES DUMARÇAY
Borobudur

JACQUES DUMARÇAY
The Temples of Java

ANNA FORBES
Unbeaten Tracks in Islands of the
Far East

GEOFFREY GORER
Bali and Angkor

JENNIFER LINDSAY
Javanese Gamelan

EDWIN M. LOEB
Sumatra: Its History and People

MOCHTAR LUBIS
The Outlaw and Other Stories

MOCHTAR LUBIS
Twilight in Djakarta

MADELON H. LULOFS
Coolie*

MADELON H. LULOFS
Rubber

COLIN McPHEE
A House in Bali*

ERIC MJOBERG
Forest Life and Adventures in the
Malay Archipelago

HICKMAN POWELL
The Last Paradise

E. R. SCIDMORE
Java, The Garden of the East

MICHAEL SMITHIES
Yogyakarta: Cultural Heart of
Indonesia

LADISLAO SZÉKELY
Tropic Fever: The Adventures of
a Planter in Sumatra

EDWARD C. VAN NESS
AND SHITA
PRAWIROHARDJO
Javanese Wayang Kulit

## MALAYSIA
ISABELLA L. BIRD
The Golden Chersonese: Travels
in Malaya in 1879

MARGARET BROOKE
THE RANEE OF
SARAWAK
My Life in Sarawak

HENRI FAUCONNIER
The Soul of Malaya

W. R. GEDDES
Nine Dayak Nights

A. G. GLENISTER
The Birds of the Malay Peninsula,
Singapore and Penang

C. W. HARRISON
Illustrated Guide to the Federated
Malay States (1923)

BARBARA HARRISSON
Orang-Utan

TOM HARRISSON
World Within: A Borneo Story

CHARLES HOSE
The Field-Book of a Jungle-Wallah

EMILY INNES
The Chersonese with the
Gilding Off

W. SOMERSET
MAUGHAM
Ah King and Other Stories*

W. SOMERSET
MAUGHAM
The Casuarina Tree*

MARY McMINNIES
The Flying Fox*

ROBERT PAYNE
The White Rajahs of Sarawak

OWEN RUTTER
The Pirate Wind

ROBERT W. SHELFORD
A Naturalist in Borneo

CARVETH WELLS
Six Years in the Malay Jungle

## SINGAPORE
RUSSELL GRENFELL
Main Fleet to Singapore

R. W. E. HARPER AND
HARRY MILLER
Singapore Mutiny

JANET LIM
Sold for Silver

G. M. REITH
Handbook to Singapore (1907)

C. E. WURTZBURG
Raffles of the Eastern Isles

## THAILAND
CARL BOCK
Temples and Elephants

REGINALD CAMPBELL
Teak-Wallah

MALCOLM SMITH
A Physician at the Court of Siam

ERNEST YOUNG
The Kingdom of the Yellow Robe

* Titles marked with an asterisk have restricted rights.